THE NOEL COWARD SONG BOOK

Books by Noël Coward

THE NOËL COWARD SONG BOOK

With an introduction and annotations
by Noël Coward

Illustrations by Gladys Calthrop

Methuen · London · New York

This edition first published
in Great Britain in 1984
by Methuen London Ltd,
11 New Fetter Lane, London EC4P 4EE

First published in paperback in the U.S.A. 1984 by
Methuen, Inc., 733 Third Avenue, New York, N.Y. 10017

The Noël Coward Song Book
originally published in 1953
by Michael Joseph Ltd

ISBN 0 413 56640 4 (Cloth)
ISBN 0 416 00961 1 (U.S. paperback edition)

Printed in Great Britain

Contents

The Forties   191

The Fifties   267

Appendix

ACKNOWLEDGMENTS are due to the following for permission to reproduce songs in this book:

To Messrs. Chappell & Company for all the songs printed in this book of which they own the copyright.

To the executors of the late Sir Charles Cochran for *A Room with a View*; *Dance Little Lady*; *World Weary*; *I'll See You Again*; *If Love Were All*; *Zigeuner*; *If You Could Only Come With Me*; *Someday I'll Find You*; *Mirabelle*; *Twentieth Century Blues*; *Half Caste Woman*; *Any Little Fish*; *I Travel Alone*; *Mrs. Worthington*; *Mad Dogs and Englishmen*; *Mad About the Boy*; *Let's Say Good-bye*; *The Party's Over Now*; *I'll Follow My Secret Heart*; *Never More*; *Regency Rakes*.

To Messrs. William Heinemann Ltd. for permission to reprint the lyrics of *A Room with a View*; *Dance Little Lady*; *World Weary*; *I'll See You Again*; *If Love Were All*; *Zigeuner*; *If You Could Only Come With Me*; *Someday I'll Find You*; *Mirabelle*; *Twentieth Century Blues*; *Mad Dogs and Englishmen*; *Mad About the Boy*; *Let's Say Good-bye*; *The Party's Over Now*; *I'll Follow My Secret Heart*; *Never More*; *Regency Rakes*; *We Were Dancing*; *You Were There*; *Play, Orchestra, Play*; *Dearest Love*; *Where Are the Songs We Sung?*; *The Stately Homes of England*.

To Messrs. Keith Prowse & Co. Ltd. for *Parisian Pierrot*.
To Messrs. Asherberg Hopwood & Crew for *Poor Little Rich Girl*.

Introduction

by NOËL COWARD

I was born into a generation that still took light music seriously. The lyrics and melodies of Gilbert and Sullivan were hummed and strummed into my consciousness at an early age. My father sang them, my mother played them, my nurse, Emma, breathed them through her teeth while she was washing me, dressing me and undressing me and putting me to bed. My aunts and uncles, who were legion, sang them singly and in unison at the slightest provocation. By the time I was four years old 'Take a Pair of Sparkling Eyes', 'Tit Willow', 'We're Very Wide Awake, the Moon and I' and 'I Have a Song to Sing-O' had been fairly inculcated into my bloodstream.

The whole Edwardian era was saturated with operetta and musical comedy: in addition to popular foreign importations by Franz Lehar, Leo Fall, André Messager, etc., our own native composers were writing musical scores of a quality that has never been equalled in this country since the 1914–18 war. Lionel Monckton, Paul Rubens, Ivan Caryll and Leslie Stuart were flourishing. 'The Quaker Girl', 'Our Miss Gibbs', 'Miss Hook of Holland', 'Florodora', 'The Arcadians' and 'The Country Girl', to name only a few, were all fine musical achievements, and over and above the artists who performed them, the librettists who wrote them and the impresarios who presented them, their music was the basis of their success. Their

9

famous and easily remembered melodies can still be heard on the radio and elsewhere, but it was in the completeness of their scores that their real strength lay: opening choruses, finales, trios, quartettes and concerted numbers—all musicianly, all well balanced and all beautifully constructed.

There was no song-plugging in those days beyond an occasional reprise in the last act; there was no assaulting of the ear by monstrous repetition, no unmannerly nagging. A little while ago I went to an American 'musical' in which the hit number was reprised no less than five times during the performance by different members of the cast, as well as being used in the overture, the entr'acte and as a 'play-out' while the audience was leaving the theatre. The other numbers in the show, several of which were charming, were left to fend for themselves and only three of them were ever published. In earlier days the complete vocal score of a musical comedy was published as a matter of course, in addition to which a booklet of the lyrics could be bought in the theatre with the programme. These little paper-bound books were well worth the sixpence charged because they helped those with a musical ear to recapture more easily the tunes they wanted to remember and to set them in their minds.

In the years immediately preceding the first world war the American Invasion began innocuously with a few isolated song hits until Irving Berlin established a beach-head with 'Alexander's Ragtime Band'. English composers, taken by surprise and startled by vital Negro-Jewish rhythms from the New World, fell back in some disorder; conservative musical opinion was shocked and horrified by such alien noises and, instead of saluting the new order and welcoming the new vitality, turned up its patrician nose and retired disgruntled from the arena.

At this moment war began, and there was no longer any time. It is reasonable to suppose that a large number of potential young composers were wiped out in those sad years and that had they not been, the annihilation of English light music would not have been so complete. As it was, when finally the surviving boys came home, it was to an occupied country; the American victory was a *fait accompli*. This obviously was the moment for British talent to rally, to profit by defeat, to absorb and utilize the new, exciting rhythms from over the water and to modify and adapt them to its own service, but apparently this was either beyond our capacity or we were too tired to attempt it. At all events, from the nineteen-twenties until today, there have been few English composers of light music capable of creating an integrated score.

One outstanding exception was the late Ivor Novello. His primary talent throughout his whole life was music, and 'Glamorous Night', 'Arc de Triomphe', 'The Dancing Years', 'Perchance to Dream' and 'King's Rhapsody' were rich in melody and technically expert. For years he upheld, almost alone, our old traditions of musical Musical Comedy. His principal tunes were designed, quite deliberately, to catch the ear of the public and, being simple, sentimental, occasionally conventional but always melodic, they invariably achieved their object. The rest of his scores, the openings, finales, choral interludes and incidental themes he wrote to please himself and in these, I believe, lay his true quality; a much finer quality than most people realized. The fact that his music never received the critical acclaim that it deserved was irritating but unimportant. One does not expect present-day dramatic critics to know much about music; as a matter of fact one no longer expects them to know much about drama. Vivian Ellis has also proved over the years that he can handle a complete score with grace and finesse. 'Bless the Bride' was much more than a few attractive songs strung together and so, from the musical standpoint, was 'Tough at the Top', although the show on the whole was a commercial failure.

Harold Fraser-Simson, who composed 'The Maid of the Mountains', and Frederic Norton, who composed 'Chu Chin Chow', are remembered only for these two outstanding scores. Their other music, later or earlier, is forgotten except by a minority.

I now arrive at the moment when willy-nilly I must discuss, as objectively as possible, my own contributions to this particular field. I have, within the last twenty-five years, composed many successful songs and three integrated scores of which I am genuinely proud. These are 'Bitter Sweet', 'Conversation Piece', and 'Pacific 1860'. 'This Year of Grace' and 'Words and Music', although revues, were also well constructed musically. 'Operette' was sadly meagre with the exception of three numbers, 'Dearest Love', 'Where are the Songs we Sung?' and 'The Stately Homes of England'. This latter, however, being a comedy quartette, relied for its success more on its lyrics than its tune. 'Ace of Clubs' contained several good songs, but could not fairly be described as a musical score. 'Sigh No More', 'On with the Dance' and 'London Calling' are outside this discussion as they were revues containing contributions from other composers. 'Bitter Sweet', the most flamboyantly successful of all my musical shows, had a full and varied score greatly enhanced by the orchestrations of Orrelana. 'Conversation Piece' was less full and varied but had considerable quality. With these two scores Miss Elsie April, to whom I dictated them, was a tremendous help to me both in transcribing and in sound musical advice. 'Pacific 1860' was, musically, my best work to date. It was carefully balanced and well constructed and imaginatively orchestrated by Ronald Binge and Mantovani. The show, as a whole, was a failure. It had been planned on a small scale, but, owing to theatre exigencies and other circumstances, had to be blown up to fit the stage of Drury Lane. The Press blasted the book, hardly mentioned the music or lyrics, and that was that. It closed after a few months.

Proceeding on the assumption that the reader of this preface is interested in the development of my musical talent, I will try to explain, as concisely as I can, how, in this respect, my personal wheels go round. To begin with, I have only had two music lessons in my life. These were the first steps of what was to have been a full course at the Guildhall School of Music, and they faltered and stopped when I was told by my instructor that I could not use consecutive fifths. He went on to explain that a gentleman called Ebenezer Prout had announced many years ago that consecutive fifths were wrong and must in no circumstances be employed. At that time Ebenezer Prout was merely a name to me (as a matter of fact he still is, and a very funny one at that) and I was unimpressed by his Victorian dicta. I argued back that Debussy and Ravel used consecutive fifths like mad. My instructor waved aside this triviality with a pudgy hand, and I left his presence for ever with the parting shot that what was good enough for Debussy and Ravel was good enough for me. This outburst of rugged individualism deprived me of much valuable knowledge, and I have never deeply regretted it for a moment. Had I intended at the outset of my career to devote all my energies to music I would have endured the necessary training cheerfully enough, but in those days I was passionately involved in the theatre; acting and writing and singing and dancing seemed of more value to my immediate progress than counterpoint and harmony. I was willing to allow the musical side of my creative talent to take care of itself. On looking back, I think that on the whole I was right. I have often been irritated in later years by my inability to write music down effectively and by my complete lack of knowledge of orchestration except by ear, but being talented from the very beginning in several different media, I was forced by common sense to make a decision. The decision I made was to try to become a good writer and actor, and to compose tunes and harmonies whenever the urge to do so became too powerful to resist.

I have never been unduly depressed by the fact that all my music has to be dictated. Many famous light composers never put so much as a crotchet on paper. To be born with a natural ear for music is a great and glorious gift. It is no occasion for pride and it has nothing to do with will-power, concentration or industry. It is either there or it isn't. What is so curious is that it cannot, in any circumstances, be wrong where one's own harmonies are concerned. Last year in New York, when I was recording 'Conversation Piece' with Lily Pons, I detected a false note in the orchestration. It happened to be in a very fully scored passage and the mistake was consequently difficult to trace. The orchestrator, the conductor and the musical producer insisted that I was wrong; only Lily Pons, who has perfect pitch, backed me up. Finally, after much argument and fiddle-faddle it was discovered that the oboe was playing an A flat instead of an A natural. The greatness and gloriousness of this gift, however, can frequently be offset by excruciating discomfort. On many occasions in my life I have had to sit smiling graciously while some well-meaning but inadequate orchestra obliges with a selection from my works. Cascades of wrong notes lacerate my nerves, a flat wind

13

instrument pierces my ear-drums, and though I continue to smile appreciatively, the smile, after a little while, becomes tortured and looks as if my mouth were filled with lemon juice.

I could not help composing tunes even if I wished to. Ever since I was a little boy they have dropped into my mind unbidden and often in the most unlikely circumstances. The 'Bitter Sweet' waltz, 'I'll See You Again', came to me whole and complete in a taxi when I was appearing in New York in 'This Year of Grace'. I was on my way home to my apartment after a matinée and had planned, as usual, to have an hour's rest and a light dinner before the evening performance. My taxi got stuck in a traffic block on the corner of Broadway and Seventh Avenue, klaxons were honking, cops were shouting and suddenly in the general din there was the melody, clear and unmistakable. By the time I got home the words of the first phrase had emerged. I played it over and over again on the piano (key of E flat as usual) and tried to rest, but I was too excited to sleep.

Oddly enough, one of the few songs I ever wrote that came to me in a setting appropriate to its content was 'Mad Dogs and Englishmen'. This was conceived and executed during a two-thousand-mile car drive from Hanoi in Tonkin to the Siamese border. True, the only white people to be seen were French, but one can't have everything.

The birth of 'I'll Follow my Secret Heart' was even more surprising. I was working on 'Conversation Piece' at Goldenhurst, my home in Kent. I had completed some odd musical phrases here and there but no main waltz theme, and I was firmly and miserably stuck. I had sat at the piano daily for hours, repeatedly trying to hammer out an original tune or even an arresting first phrase, and nothing had resulted from my concentrated efforts but banality. I knew that I could never complete the score without my main theme as a pivot and finally, after ten days' increasing despair, I decided to give up and, rather than go on flogging myself any further, postpone the whole project for at least six months. This would entail telegraphing to Yvonne Printemps who was in Paris waiting eagerly for news and telling Cochran who had already announced the forthcoming production in the Press. I felt fairly wretched but at least relieved that I had had the sense to admit failure while there was still time. I poured myself a large whisky and soda, dined in grey solitude, poured myself another, even larger, whisky and soda, and sat gloomily envisaging everybody's disappointment and facing the fact that my talent had withered and that I should never write any more music until the day I died. The whisky did little to banish my gloom, but there was no more work to be done and I didn't care if I became fried as a coot, so I gave myself another drink and decided to go to bed. I switched off the lights at the door and noticed that there was one lamp left on by the piano. I walked automatically to turn it off, sat down and played 'I'll Follow my Secret Heart', straight through in G flat, a key I had never played in before.

There is, to me, strange magic in such occurrences. I am willing and delighted to accept praise for my application, for my self-discipline and for my grim determination to finish a thing once I have started it. My acquired knowledge is praiseworthy, too, for I have worked hard all my life to perfect the material at my disposal. But these qualities, admirable as they undoubtedly are, are merely accessories. The essential talent is what matters and essential talent is unexplainable. My mother and father were both musical in a light, amateur sense, but their gift was in no way remarkable. My father, although he could improvise agreeably at the piano, never composed a set piece of music in his life. I have known many people who were tone-deaf whose parents were far more actively musical than mine. I had no piano lessons when I was a little boy except occasionally from my mother who tried once or twice, with singular lack of success, to teach me my notes. I could, however, from the age of about seven onwards, play any tune I had heard on the piano in the pitch dark. To this day my piano-playing is limited to three keys: E flat, B flat and A flat. The sight of two sharps frightens me to death. When I am in the process of composing anything in the least complicated I can play it in any key on the keyboard, but I can seldom if ever repeat these changes afterwards unless I practise them assiduously every day. In E flat I can give the impression of playing well. A flat and B flat I can get away with, but if I have to play anything for the first time it is always to my beloved E flat that my fingers move automatically. Oddly enough, C major, the key most favoured by the inept, leaves me cold. It is supposed to be easier to play in than any of the others because it has no black notes, but I have always found it dull. Another of my serious piano-playing defects is my left hand. Dear George Gershwin used to moan at me in genuine distress and try to force my fingers on to the right notes. As a matter of fact he showed me a few tricks that I can still do, but they are few and dreadfully far between. I can firmly but not boastfully claim that I am a better pianist than Irving Berlin, but as that superlative genius of light music is well known not to be able to play at all except in C major, I will not press the point. Jerome D. Kern, to my mind one of the most inspired romantic composers of all, played woodenly as a rule and without much mobility. Dick Rodgers plays his own music best when he is accompanying himself or someone else, but he is far from outstanding. Vincent Youmans was a marvellous pianist, almost as brilliant as Gershwin, but these are the only two I can think of who, apart from their creative talent, could really play.

At the very beginning of this introduction I said that I was born into a generation that took light music seriously. It was fortunate for me that I was, because by the time I had emerged from my teens the taste of the era had changed. In my early twenties and thirties it was from America that I gained my greatest impetus. In New York they have always taken light music seriously There, it is, as it should be, saluted as a specialized form of creative art, and is secure in its own right. The basis of a successful American musical show is now and has been for many years its music and its lyrics. Here in England there are few to write the music and fewer still to recognize it when it is written. The commercial managers have to fill their vast theatres and prefer, naturally enough, to gamble on acknowledged Broadway successes rather than questionable home products. The critics are quite incapable of distinguishing between good light music and bad light music, and the public are so saturated with the cheaper outpourings of Tin Pan Alley, which are dinned into their ears interminably by the B.B.C., that their natural taste will soon die a horribly unnatural death. It is a depressing thought, but perhaps some day soon, someone, somewhere, will appear with an English musical so strong in native quality that it will succeed in spite of the odds stacked against it. This handsome volume contains fifty-one of my songs. They are divided into sections according to the years in which they were composed. Each section is prefaced by a further little introductory note. The book therefore not only contains far too many songs but far too many little introductory notes, so I will bring this preliminary canter to a close with the hope that I have not bored the reader with a too detailed analysis of my musical abilities.

The Twenties

Forbidden Fruit In the words of this song, written when I was sixteen, the worldly cynicism of which I have so often been accused in later years is already seen to be rearing its ugly head. A precocious recognition of the fallibility of human behaviour is immediately apparent in the first three lines of the verse

> 'Ordinary man
> Invariably sighs
> Vainly for what cannot be.'

Things go from bad to worse in the refrain which, although it begins fairly skittishly with the objective statement 'Every peach out of reach is attractive', ends on a note of bitter disillusion

> 'For the brute
> Loves the fruit
> That's forbidden
> And I'll bet you half a crown
> He'll appreciate the flavour of it much much more
> If he has to climb a bit to shake it down.'

True, the suggested wager of half a crown rather lets down the tone. One cannot help feeling that a bet of fifty pounds, or at least a fiver, would be more in keeping with the general urbanity of the theme:

19

for a brief moment the veneer is scratched and Boodle's, White's and Buck's are elbowed aside by the Clapham Tennis Club, but this perhaps is hyper-criticism and it must also be remembered that to the author half a crown in 1916 was the equivalent of five pounds in 1926. Also, it rhymes with 'down'. At all events, 'Forbidden Fruit' was the first completely integrated song I ever wrote and for this reason it is included in this book.

Parisian Pierrot

From 'London Calling', 1923. This song, sung enchantingly by Gertrude Lawrence in 'London Calling', has always been one of my favourites. The idea of it came to me in a night club in Berlin in 1922. A frowsy blonde, wearing a sequin chest-protector and a divided skirt, appeared in the course of the cabaret with a rag pierrot doll dressed in black velvet. She placed it on a cushion where it sprawled in pathetic abandon while she pranced round it emitting guttural noises. Her performance was unimpressive but the doll fascinated me. The title 'Parisian Pierrot' slipped into my mind, and, in the taxi on the way back to my hotel, the song began.

Poor Little Rich Girl

From 'On With the Dance', 1925. This was my first authentic song hit. By this I mean that it sold many more copies than anything else I had written, and was played by dance bands all over London. It had a stormy career. In the first place, Charles Cochran wanted to throw it out of the revue 'On With the Dance' during the try-out in Manchester. I fought like a steer for it and so, fortunately, did Alice Delysia, who sang it. She considered it, rightly I think, to be her best number in the show. It was led up to by a sophisticated little scene played by Hermione Baddeley who stood about in evening dress looking drained and far from healthy, while Delysia, as her French governess, lectured her in a worldly manner about the debauched life she was all too obviously leading. Later, after the original battle had been fought and won by Delysia and me and the song was an established success, there was a further battle between Cochran and me because Gertie Lawrence wanted to sing it in the second Charlot revue in New York. After much acrimonious correspondence and threats of injunctions, etc., Gertie sang it dressed as a tart with a white fox fur. Constance Carpenter was the Poor Little Rich Girl in question and stood about in evening-dress, looking drained and far from healthy. It was a hit in New York also, and the years dissipated the last vestige of ill-feeling between Cochran and me.

A Room With a View
★
Dance, Little Lady

From 'This Year of Grace', 1928. 'A Room With a View' was originally conceived on a lonely beach in Honolulu where I was convalescing after a nervous breakdown. The title, unblushingly pinched from E. M. Forster's novel, came into my mind together with a musical phrase to fit it and I splashed up and down in the shallows, searching for shells and rhymes at the same time. When I was singing it in the American production of 'This Year of Grace' the late Alexander Woollcott took a black hatred to it. The last couplet:

'Maybe a stork will bring, this that and t'other thing to
Our room with a view'

sent him into transports of vituperation. He implored me to banish the number from the show or at least promise not to sing it myself, and when I refused to pander to his wicked prejudices he decided to make a more public protest. One evening he came to the Selwyn Theatre and sat in a stage box with a group of ramshackle companions, including Harpo Marx, and when I began to sing the verse they all, with one accord, ostentatiously opened newspapers and read them. My voice faltered and stopped and I broke down in helpless giggles. After a while I rallied and, with what I still consider to be great presence of mind, sang the last couplet in baby talk, whereupon Woollcott gave a dreadful scream and, making sounds only too indicative of rising nausea, staggered from the box. The audience, I fear, was a trifle bewildered.

21

In the original production in London the song was sung by Jessie Matthews and Sonnie Hale looking out of a window. 'Dance Little Lady' was also sung by Sonnie Hale in London and by me in New York. It was danced respectively by Lauri Devine and Florence Desmond. They both wore evening dress and looked drained and far from healthy, and were surrounded by a macabre group of 'Bright Young Things' wearing Oliver Messel masks. The high tone of moral indignation implicit in the lyric impressed a number of people, notably the late Aimée Semple Macpherson.

World Weary

'World Weary' was sung by Beatrice Lillie in the American production of 'This Year of Grace'. She sang it dressed as an office boy, sitting on a high stool while munching an apple realistically, sometimes at the expense of the lyric. Recently I sang it myself at the Café de Paris wearing an alpaca dinner jacket and not munching an apple. The penultimate couplet:

'I can hardly wait, Till I see the great, Open spaces—
My loving friends will not be there, I'm so sick of their God-damned faces'

had to be changed for the published edition. 'Gosh darned' was substituted for 'God-damned'. This compromise, while soothing outraged public opinion, weakened the song considerably.

I'll See You Again
*
If Love Were All
*
Zigeuner*

These four songs are all from 'Bitter Sweet', 1929. 'If Love Were All' was sung by Ivy St. Helier with exquisite pathos in the first scene of the second act. 'Zigeuner' was originally sung by Peggy Wood and later by Evelyn Laye, in the first scene of the third act. 'If You Could Only Come With Me' which, in the operette, immediately precedes 'I'll See You Again', was sung by George Metaxa, and remains to date one of my own favourite compositions. 'I'll See You Again', I am happy to say, has been sung incessantly by everybody. It has proved over the years to be the greatest song

Bitter Sweet

If You Could Only Come With Me hit I have ever had or am ever likely to have. I have heard it played in all parts of the world. Brass bands have blared it, string orchestras have swooned it, Palm Court quartettes have murdered it, barrel organs have ground it out in London squares and swing bands have tortured it beyond recognition. It is as popular today as when it was first heard, and I am still fond of it and very proud of it.

'Bitter Sweet' ended my musical output of the nineteen-twenties.

Forbidden Fruit
[Every Peach]

1. Or-din-a-ry man in - var-i-a-bly sighs
2. If a man's engaged and feels that he is loved,
3. Wo-men haven't al - tered since the days of Eve,

Vain-ly for what can - not be,
Bla-sé he will quick - ly be,
Anx-ious-ly through life they prowl,

If he's in an or - chard
Of - ten on one side his
Always trying to bet - ter

he will cast his eyes
la - dy - love is shoved
what their friends a - chieve,

Up in - to the high - est tree,
While he goes up - on the spree.
Ei - ther by fair means or foul.

A

There may be a lot of wind-falls Ly - ing all a - round But you'll
Then per - haps she'll mar - ry____ And you can bet your life____ He'll
girl may be quite care - ful Of the sort of life she picks, But to

nev - er see a man en - joy the fruit that's on the ground.
want her ver - y bad - ly when she's some - one else - 's wife.
be a real suc - cess she's got to know a lot of tricks.

REFRAIN

1. Ev - 'ry peach out of reach is at - trac - tive 'Cos it's
2. Ev - 'ry peach out of reach is at - trac - tive 'Cos it's
3. Ev - 'ry peach out of reach is at - trac - tive 'Cos it's

mf

l.h.

just a lit - tle bit too high,
just a lit - tle bit too high,
just a lit - tle bit too high,

And you'll find that ev - 'ry man Will try to
Though it is - n't ve - ry sane To make the
Ev - en well brought-up young girls Will look at

26

pluck it if he can   As he pass - es   by.   For a
things you can't at-tain,   Still you al - ways   try.   If you
oth - er women's pearls   With a yearn - ing   eye.   If they

brute loves the fruit   that's for-bid - den   And I'll bet you   half a
find   that you're blind   with de - vo - tion   For de - light - ful Mrs. ___
fight day and night   per - se - ver - ing   And a   small string they col -

l.h.

crown   He'll ap - pre - ci - ate the fla-vour of   it   much much more   If he
Brown,   You'll ap - pre - ci - ate   e - lop - ing with her much much more   If her
-lect,   They'll ap - pre - ci - ate the col - our of them much much more   If they'd

1   **2**
has to climb a bit   to shake it down.   Ev-'ry   down.
husband comes along and knocks you down.   Ev-'ry   down.
sac - ri - ficed a lit - tle self - re-spect.   Ev-'ry   -spect.

f   *fz*

Parisian Pierrot

from

LONDON CALLING

Fan - ta - sy in old - en days In
Mourn-ful-ness has al - ways been The

var - y - ing and dif-f'rent ways, Was ve - ry much in vogue,
key-note of a Pier-rot scene When Pas-sion plays a part,

Col - um - bine and Pan - ta - loon, A wist - ful Pier - rot 'neath the moon, And
Pier - rot in a tra - gic pose Will kiss a fa - ded sil - ver rose, With

Har - le-quin a rogue.
sad-ness in his heart.

Now - a - days Par-is - i - ans of
Some day soon he'll leave his tears be -

leis - ure,
-hind him,

Wake the ec - ho of an old re - frain,
Com - e - dy comes laugh-ing down the street,

Each some rag - ged ef - fi - gy will trea - sure for his plea - sure, Till the
Col - um-bine will fly to him, ad - mir - ing and de - sir - ing, lay - ing

shad - ows of their sto - ry live a - gain. Par - is - i - an
love and ad - or - a - tion at his feet. Par - is - i - an

REFRAIN

Pier-rot_____ So-ci-e-ty's he-ro_____ The Lord of a day, The Rue de la Paix Is un-der your sway,_____ The world may flat-ter_____ But what does that mat-ter,_____ They'll nev-er shat-ter_____ your gloom pro-found,_____ Par-is-i-an Pier-rot_____ your spir-it's at ze-ro,_____

Di - vine-ly for - lorn, With ex-quis-ite scorn, From sun-set to dawn,

The lim-bo is call - ing, Your star will be fall - ing,

As soon as the clock goes round. Par-is - i-an

1

2

round.

31

Poor Little Rich Girl

from

CHARLOT'S REVUE OF 1926

1. You're on-ly a ba-by,
2. The role you are act-ing,

You're lone-ly, and may-be Some-day soon you'll know
The toll is ex-act-ing; Soon you'll have to pay.

The tears you are tast-ing Are years you are wast-ing, Life's a bit - ter
The mus - ic of liv-ing You lose in the giv-ing, False things soon de -

foe. With fate it's no use com-pet - ing,
- cay. These words from me may sur - prise you,

Youth is so ter - ri-bly fleet - ing; By danc-ing much fast-er,
I've got no right to ad - vise you, I've known life too well, dear,

You're chancing dis - as - ter, Time a - lone will show.
Your own life must tell, dear, Please don't turn a - way.

33

REFRAIN Steady rhythm

Poor lit - tle rich girl, You're a be - witched girl,

Bet - ter be-ware!

Laugh - ing at dan - ger, Vir - tue a stran - ger,

Bet-ter take care!

The life you lead sets all your nerves a - jan - gle,

Your love af - fairs are in a hope - less tan - gle,

Though you're a child, dear, Your life's a wild ty -

phoon,

In lives of leis - ure, The craze for pleas - ure, stead-i - ly grows.

Cock - tails and

laugh - ter But what comes af - ter? No-bod-y knows.

You're weav-ing

ff

love in - to a mad jazz pat-tern, Ruled by pan-ta -

-loon. _____ Poor lit-tle rich girl, don't drop a

stitch too soon.

soon.

A Room with a View

from

COCHRAN'S 1928 REVUE

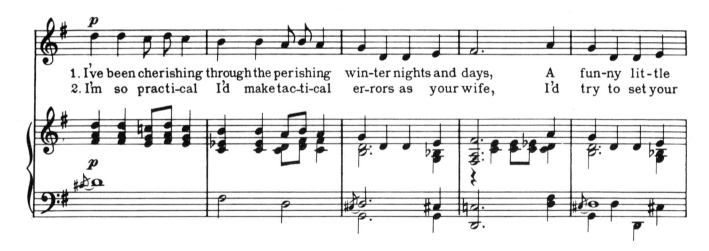

1. I've been cherishing through the perishing win-ter nights and days, A fun-ny lit-tle
2. I'm so practi-cal I'd make tac-ti-cal er-rors as your wife, I'd try to set your

phrase that means_____ Such a lot to me that you've got to be
life to rights._____ I'm up-set a bit for I get a bit

with me heart and soul   For on you the whole thing leans. ____
diz-zy now and then   Fol-low-ing the men-tal flights ____

Won't you kind-ly tell me what you're driv-ing at, ____ What con-clu-
Come with me and leave be-hind the noi-sy crowds, ____ Sun-light shines

- sion you're ar-riv-ing at? ____ Please don't turn a-way or my dream will stay
____ for us a-bove the clouds. ____ My eyes glistened too while I listened to

hid-den out of sight A-mong a lot of might-have-beens.
all the things you said, I'm glad I've got a head for heights.

rit.

39

REFRAIN

A Room with a View, and you, and no one to wor - ry us,
View, and you, and no one to give ad-vice,

no one to hur -ry us through this dream we've found. We'll gaze at the
That sounds a par - a-dise few could fail to choose. With fin-gers en -

sky, and try to guess what it's all a-bout, then we will fig-ure out
-twined we'll find re - lief from the preachers who al -ways be-seech us to

why the world is round. We'll be as hap - py and con -
mind our P's and Q's We'll watch the whole world pass be -

40

-tent - ed   as   birds   up-on   a   tree   High   a - bove   the   moun-tains   and
-fore us   while   we   are sit - ting still,   Lean-ing   on   our   own   win -   dow

sea._____   We'll   bill__   and we'll   coo -   ooo - oo   And
sill._____   We'll   bill__   and we'll   coo -   ooo - oo   And

sor - row will nev - er come,   Oh, will it ev - er come   true _____   our room with a
may - be   a stork will bring   this, that and t'other thing to _____   our room with a

view?   A Room with a   view._____

rit.

41

Dance Little Lady
from
THIS YEAR OF GRACE

Though you're on-ly sev-en-teen far too much of life you've seen, syn-co-pa - ted child.

May-be if you on-ly knew where your path is lead-ing to

you'd be-come less wild; But I know it's vain

try-ing to ex-plain while there's this in-sane mu-sic in your

Tempo I REFRAIN

brain. Dance, dance, dance, lit-tle la-dy!

Youth is fleet - ing to the rhy - thm beat - ing In your mind.

43

Dance, dance, dance, lit-tle la-dy, so ob-sessed_ with sec-ond best, no rest_ you'll ev-er find._____ Time and tide and trou-ble nev-er, nev-er wait, Let the caul-dron bub-ble, Just-i-fy your fate. Dance, dance, dance, lit-tle la-dy! Dance, dance, dance, lit-tle la-dy!

Leave to-mor-row be - hind.

When the sax - o-phone gives a wick-ed moan, Charles-ton_ Hey! Hey!

Rhy - thms_ fall and_ rise. Start danc-ing

to the tune_ the band's croon-ing_ for soon the night_ will be gone.

Start sway-ing like a reed_ with-out heed-ing the speed that hur-

-ries you on. Nig-ger mel-o-dies syn-co-pate_ your nerves

till your bo-dy curves, Droop-ing__ stoop-ing.__

Laugh-ter_ some day_ dies,_____ And when the

lights are start - ing to gut - ter   Dawn through the shut - ter

shows you're liv - ing in a world of lies.

REFRAIN
Tempo I

Dance, dance, dance, lit -tle la - dy! Youth is fleet - ing to the

rhy - thm beat - ing in your mind.

Dance, dance, dance, lit-tle la - dy, so ob - sessed___ with sec - ond

best, no rest___ you'll ev - er find._____

Time and tide and trou - ble nev - er, nev - er wait,

Let the caul - dron bub - ble, Just - i - fy your fate.

Dance, dance, dance, lit-tle la - dy! Dance, dance, dance, lit-tle la - dy!

Leave your trou - bles be - hind.

- hind.

ff allargando

cresc.

sfz

Fine

49

World Weary
from
THIS YEAR OF GRACE

Moderato

mf

p

p *dim. e rit.* *p a tempo*

1 When I'm feel - ing drear - y and
2 Get up in the morn - ing at

blue I'm on - ly too glad to be left a -
eight, Re - lent - less fate Drives me to work at

p

-lone, Dream - ing of a place in the
nine; Toil - ing like a bee in a

p

sun when day is done, Far from the tel - e - phone;
hive From four to five, Wheth - er it's wet or fine,

Bus - tle and the wear - y crowd,
Hard - ly ev - er see the sky,

Make me want to cry out loud. Give me something peaceful and
Build-ings seem to grow so high. May - be in the fu - ture I

grand Where all the land slum - bers in mo - no - tone I'm
will Per - haps ful - fil This lit - tle dream of mine. I'm

51

REFRAIN (not fast)

world wear-y,   world wear-y,   Liv-ing in a great big   town;___ I find it
world wear-y,   world wear-y,   Liv-ing in a great big   town;___ I find it

so drear-y,   so drear-y,   Ev-'rything looks grey or   brown.___ I want an o-cean blue,
so drear-y,   so drear-y,   Ev-'rything looks grey or   brown.___ I want a horse and plough,

great big trees, A bird's eye view of the Py-re-nees; I want to watch the moon rise
chick-ens too,   Just one cow with a wist-ful moo. A coun-try where the verb "to

up___ And see the great red sun go   down.   Watching clouds go by through a
work"   Becomes a most im-prop-er   noun.   I can hard-ly wait 'Till I

52

win-try sky fas - cin - ates me, But if I'm stand-ing in the street Ev-'ry
see the great op - en spac - es, My lov - ing friends will not be there I'm so

one I meet sim-ply hates me,___ Be-cause I'm world wear-y, world wear-y,
sick of their gol-darned fac - es,___ Be-cause I'm world wear-y, world wear-y,

p

I could kiss the rail-road tracks, I want to get right back to na - ture and re -
Tired of all these jumping jacks, I want to get right back to na - ture and re -

poco rit.

-lax. I'm
-lax.

a tempo

mf

sf

Ped.

53

I'll See You Again

from
BITTER SWEET

(He) Now, Miss Sar-ah, if you please, Sing a scale for me. *(She)* Ah ———

(He) Take a breath and then re - prise in a dif - f'rent key.

(She) Ah ⸻

(He) All my life I shall re- -mem - ber know-ing you; All the plea-sure I have found in show-ing you

Ah ⸻ Ah ⸻

The dif - f'rent ways That one may phrase,

The chang-ing light and chang-ing shade,

Hap-pi-ness that must die, Mel-o-dies that must fly, Mem-o-ries that must

(She) Ah _____ fade Dus-ty and for-got-ten by and by. _____

(She) Learn - ing scales will nev-er seem so sweet a-gain Till our

des-ti-ny shall let us meet a-gain. Ah _____

The will of fate

Ah _____ When I'm re - call - ing the hours we've

May come too late.

had Why will the fool - ish tears Trem - ble a - cross the

years? Why shall I feel so sad, Trea - sur - ing the

Ah _____

mem - 'ry of these days _____ al - ways? _____

Tempo di Valse

I'll see you a - gain When-ev-er spring breaks

I'll see you a - gain When-ev-er spring breaks

through a - gain. Time may lie heav- y be - tween, _____ But what has

through a - gain. Time may lie heav- y be - tween, _____ But what has

been _____ is past for - get - ting. This sweet mem - o -

been _____ is past for - get - ting. This sweet mem - o -

-ry A-cross the years will come to me; Tho'my world may go a-

-ry A-cross the years will come to me;

-wry, In my heart will ev-er lie Just the ech-o of a sigh, good-

Just the ech-o of a sigh, good-

-bye. sigh, good - bye!

-bye. sigh, good - bye!

If Love Were All

from

BITTER SWEET

Assai moderato

p

poco espressivo

mf

poco rall.

p

p a tempo

Life is ve - ry rough and tum - ble For a hum - ble   di - seuse;
Tho' life buf - fets me ob - scene - ly   It se - rene - ly   goes   on;

One can be - tray one's trou - bles nev - er,   What - ev - er   oc - curs.
Al - tho' I ques - tion its con - clu - sion,   Il - lu - sion   is   gone.

Night af - ter night   have to look bright   Whe-ther you're well or   ill;
Fre-quent-ly I   put a bit by   Safe for a rain-y   day.

Peo-ple must laugh their   fill____ You must-n't   sleep__ till dawn comes creep - ing.
No-bo-dy here can   say____ To what in - deed__ the years are   lead - ing.

Tho' I nev-er real - ly grum-ble, Life's a jum - ble   in - deed_____
Fate may of - ten treat me mean-ly, But I keen - ly   pur - sue,_____

__ And in my ef-forts to suc-ceed _____ I've had to form-u - late a   creed.__
__ A lit-tle mi-rage in the blue._____ De-ter-min-a - tion helps me through.

61

REFRAIN (*plaintively*)

I be-lieve in do-ing what I can, In cry-ing when I must, in laugh-ing when I choose.

Heigh - o,_____ If love were all____ I should be lone - ly. I be-lieve the

more you love a man. The more you give your trust, The more you're bound to lose: Al - though

_ when sha-dows fall____ I think if on - ly Some - bo - dy splen-did real - ly

62

need-ed me,   Some-one af-fec-tion-ate and dear,   Cares would be end-ed if   I

knew that he   Want-ed to have me near.   But I be-lieve that since my life be-gan The

most I've had is just   a   tal-ent to a-muse.   Heigh - o, ____ If love were all.

all. ____

Zigeuner

from

BITTER SWEET

Tempo di Valse

1. Once up-on a time, ____ Ma - ny years a - go, ____ Lived a fair Prin - cess Hat - ing to con - fess Lone - li - ness was tor - tur - ing her so. ___

2. Bid my weep-ing cease, ____ Mel - o - dy that brings ____ Mer - ci - ful re - lease, Prom - is - es of peace; Through the gen - tle throb-bing of the strings. __

Then a gip - sy came,
Mu - sic of the plain,

Called to her by
Mu - sic of the

name,
wild,

Woo'd her with a song
Come to me a - gain,

Sen - su - ous and
Hear me not in

cresc.

strong. All the sum-mer long Her pas-sion seemed to trem-ble like a liv-ing
vain. Soothe a heart in pain And let me to my hap-pi-ness be re-con-

frame.
-ciled.

accel.

f

65

REFRAIN

Play to me be-neath the sum-mer moon, Zi - geu - ner! - Zi-geu - ner! - Zi-geu - ner! All I ask of life is just to lis-ten To the songs that you sing__ My spi-rit like a bird on the wing__ __Your mel-o-dies a - dor - ing - soar - ing. Call to me with some bar-

-bar - ic tune, Zi - geu - - ner!— Zi - geu - - ner!— Zi-

a tempo

- geu - - ner! Now you hold me in your power

Play to me for just an hour, Zi - geu - - - - ner!

1

2

- - ner!

D.C

Ped. *

67

If You Could Only Come With Me

from
BITTER SWEET

Though there may be beau-ty in this land of yours. Skies are ver-y oft-en dull and grey. If I could but take that lit-tle hand of yours Just to lead you se-cret-ly a - way.

We would watch the Dan-ube as it gent-ly flows. Like a sil-ver rib-bon wind-ing free

Ev-en as I speak of it my longing grows. Once a-gain my own dear land to see

If you could on-ly come with me   If you could on-ly come with me.

69

The Thirties

Some Day
I'll Find You

'Some Day I'll Find You' was written as a theme song for 'Private Lives'. Gertrude Lawrence sang a refrain of it alone in the first act and in the second we sang it together. For me the memory of her standing on that moonlit stage balcony in a dead-white Molyneux dress will never fade. She was the epitome of grace and charm and imperishable glamour. I have seen many actresses play Amanda in 'Private Lives'—some brilliantly, some moderately and one or two abominably. But the part was written for Gertie and, as I conceived it and wrote it, I can say with authority that no actress in the world ever could or ever will come within a mile of her performance of it. 'Some Day I'll Find You', among my sentimental songs, ranks next in popularity to 'I'll See You Again' and, now that Gertie is no longer alive, I find the nostalgia of it almost unbearable.

Twentieth
Century
Blues
★
The
Mirabelle
Waltz

Both of these songs were sung in 'Cavalcade', 1931, the former by Binnie Barnes and the latter by Strella Wilson. The Mirabelle Waltz was really written as a satire on the popular musical comedy waltzes of the period, i.e. 1900. The words are deliberately trite and so is the tune, but it has a certain charm I think. It was utterly ruined for me because of a hitch that occurred on the opening night of the play at Drury Lane. One of the hydraulic lifts stuck during a quick

71

change and this change, which should have been effected in thirty seconds, lasted for nine minutes. To fill in that bleak eternity the musical director played the waltz over and over again. No member of that audience, with or without musical ear, could possibly have failed to remember that pretty, pretty melody. It must be embedded in their very souls. Many years passed before I could listen to it without a shudder.

Twentieth Century Blues

'Twentieth Century Blues' is ironic in theme and musically rather untidy. It is also exceedingly difficult to sing, but in the play it achieved its purpose. It struck the required note of harsh discordancy and typified, within its frame, the curious, hectic desperation I wished to convey.

Half Caste Woman

★

Any Little Fish

Both these songs were in 'Cochran's 1931 Revue' at the London Pavilion. This revue was a failure and only ran for a few weeks. 'Any Little Fish', originally sung by Ada May, achieved a certain success. 'Half Caste Woman', also sung by Ada May, did not. Later on Helen Morgan did it in New York, also in a flop. As I never heard either her or Ada May sing it I can evade comparisons. My own recording of it is only adequate. I don't think, on the whole, that poor 'Half Caste Woman' ever had a fair deal. 'Any Little Fish', on the other hand, I have always found very useful. It is bright and snappy and over quickly, and when sung with sufficient grimaces and innuendoes it can be quite tolerably suggestive.

I Travel Alone

'I Travel Alone' was never in any revue or musical comedy. I wrote it and recorded it a trifle morosely and it sold, I believe, fairly well. I liked it at the time, but not to excess. It is one of the songs that people suddenly ask for at parties, not from any passionate desire to hear it but merely to prove their cleverness in remembering that I wrote it.

Mad Dogs and Englishmen

Mrs. Worthington

This song has achieved considerable fame and has been a staunch and reliable friend to me. Throughout my concert tour in the Dominions and at troop shows from Scapa Flow to the jungles of Burma it has never failed me. It has never formed part of any score or been performed in any stage production; it has seldom been sung by anyone but me and I have only made one rather scurried recording of it. Its universal appeal lies, I believe, in its passionate sincerity. It is a genuine *cri de cœur* and as such cannot fail to ring true. Unhappily, its effectiveness, from the point of view of propaganda, has been negligible. I had hoped, by writing it, to discourage misguided maternal ambition, to deter those dreadful eager mothers from making beasts of themselves, boring the hell out of me and wasting their own and my time, but I have not succeeded. On the contrary, the song seems to have given them extra impetus and ninety-nine out of a hundred of the letters they write to me refer to it with roguish indulgence, obviously secure in the conviction that it could not in any circumstances apply to them. This is saddening, of course, but realizing that the road of the social reformer is paved with disillusion I have determined to rise above it.

Mad Dogs and Englishmen
★
Mad About the Boy
★
Let's Say Good-Bye
★
The Party's Over Now

These four numbers were in my revue 'Words and Music' which Charles B. Cochran produced at the Adelphi Theatre in 1932.

'Mad Dogs and Englishmen' was originally sung a year or two before in America by Beatrice Lillie in 'The Little Show'. In 'Words and Music' Romney Brent sang it as a missionary in one of Britain's tropical colonies. Since then I have sung it myself *ad nauseam*. On one occasion it achieved international significance. This was a dinner party given by Mr. Winston Churchill on board H.M.S. *Prince of Wales* in honour of President Roosevelt on the evening following the signing of the Atlantic Charter. From an eye-witness description of the scene it appears that the two world leaders became involved in a heated argument as to whether 'In Bankok at twelve o'clock they foam at the mouth and run' came at the end of the first refrain or at the end of the second. President Roosevelt held firmly to the latter view and refused to budge even under the impact of

Churchillian rhetoric. In this he was right and when, a little while later, I asked Mr. Churchill about the incident he admitted defeat like a man.

'Mad About the Boy'. was presented in a composite vocal scene. A society lady, a street-walker, a schoolgirl and a scullery maid in turn sang their impression of a famous film star. The singers were Joyce Barbour, Steffi Duna, Norah Howard and Doris Hare. The film star, who appeared briefly at the end, was played by Edward Underdown. I have always been very attached to this number. The refrain remains constant, with different lyrics, but the verses vary and are, I think, musically interesting, particularly the 'school-girl' verse which is begun against an accompaniment of five-finger exercises. 'Let's Say Good-Bye' was the forerunner of several songs in the same genre: 'Thanks For the Memory', 'Let's Call It a Day', 'It Was Swell While it Lasted', etc. Its emphasis is on the transience of physical passion :—

> 'Let's look on love as a plaything,
> All these sweet moments we've known
> Mustn't be degraded
> When the thrill of them has faded
> Let's say good-bye—and leave it alone.'

Wise advice indeed but not in strict accordance with the views of the Church of England.

'The Party's Over Now' is a light sentimental number which led up to the finale of the revue. In recent years I have used it as a signing-off tune at the end of my performance at the Café de Paris. It is a pleasant little song without being startlingly original.

I'll Follow My Secret Heart
★
Nevermore

From 'Conversation Piece', 1934. I have already explained in the introduction the curious circumstances in which 'I'll Follow My Secret Heart' came to be written. The other two songs from 'Conversation Piece' included in this volume are 'Nevermore' and 'Regency Rakes'. Both 'Secret Heart' and 'Nevermore' were composed for and sung by the incomparable Yvonne Printemps. It was my privilege while appearing with her in the play to listen to her every night. It is a privilege that I shall always be grateful for and a deep musical pleasure that I shall never forget. In later years, when the operette was recorded in New York, Lily Pons sang the role enchantingly. It would not only be invidious but foolish to attempt to draw comparisons between the two. Their voices and their performances were completely different. Any similarity between the two begins and ends with the fact that they are both exquisite singers and both French.

Regency Rakes

'Regency Rakes' is a robust 'Period' quartette and was led, in the original production, by a tall, handsome young man who later achieved fame as a film star. I engaged him at an audition at His Majesty's Theatre, London, in 1934. His name was George Saunders.

We Were Dancing
★
You Were There
★
Play, Orchestra, Play

From 'To-night at Eight-Thirty', 1936. 'To-night at Eight-Thirty' was a series of nine short plays conceived and written for Gertrude Lawrence and myself. We played them on consecutive evenings, three plays to a performance. 'We Were Dancing' was the title of the opening play of the first series. It was light in texture, hardly more than a sketch. Gertie and I sang the number very quickly indeed with little vocal prowess but considerable abandon. Fortunately the audiences appeared to enjoy it.

'Play, Orchestra, Play' and 'You Were There' were both in 'Shadow Play', the last play of the second series, a romantic fantasy concerning the breaking up and coming together again of a young married couple. At the end of the first scene of the play we belted out 'Play, Orchestra, Play' in the teeth of the audience while the stage staff was changing the scene behind us. 'You Were There' we sang and danced more tranquilly in a moonlit garden. It was reprised by me later in the show while Gertie was scrambling breathlessly into a grey bouffant dress in the quick-change room at the side of the stage. It is a pleasant, sentimental little song and we both enjoyed doing it.

75

Dearest Love
★
Where Are The Songs We Sung?
★
The Stately Homes of England

From 'Operette', 1938. 'Dearest Love' and 'Where Are The Songs We Sung?' were both sung charmingly by Peggy Wood and are both, I think, attractive songs. Musically speaking, the verse of the latter is unusual and offsets the conventionality of the refrain.

'The Stately Homes of England' was what is colloquially known as a 'show stopper'. It was performed by Hugh French, John Gatrell, Angus Menzies and Ross Landon. They were all nice looking, their diction was clear and they never went off without resounding applause. Since then I have recorded it and sung it all over the world and it has been popular with everyone with the exception of a Mayoress in New Zealand who said it let down the British Empire.

Never Again

This song was written for the American edition of 'Words and Music' ('Set to Music'), Music Box Theatre, New York, 1939. It was sung in that production by a Spanish lady called Eva Ortega who evaded the worldly cynicism implicit in the lyric by the cunning device of singing it quite unintelligibly. Her voice, however, was very resonant. Much later, in 1945, it was sung, clearly, by Graham Payn in 'Sigh No More' at the Piccadilly Theatre.

I Went to a Marvellous Party

From 'Set to Music', 1939. During the summer of 1937 or 1938, I forget which, Elsa Maxwell gave a party in the South of France. It was a 'Beach' party and when she invited Grace Moore, Beatrice Lillie and me she explained that we were to 'come as we were' and that it would be 'just ourselves'. When we arrived (as we were) we discovered that 'just ourselves' meant about a hundred of us, all in the last stages of evening dress. We also discovered that one of the objects of the party was for us to entertain. As we were on holiday and had no accompanist and were not in any way prepared to perform, we refused. Elsa was perfectly understanding, but the other guests were a trifle disgruntled. I believe Beattie was persuaded to sing, but Grace and I held firm. This whole glittering episode was my original inspiration for 'I went to a Marvellous Party'. Beattie eventually sang the song in 'Set to Music' wearing slacks, a fisherman's shirt, several ropes of pearls, a large sun-hat and dark glasses. She has sung it a great deal since.

Conversation Piece

Someday I'll Find You

from
PRIVATE LIVES

1. When one is lone-ly the days are long; You seem so
2. Can't you re-mem-ber the fun we had? Time is so

near, But nev-er ap-pear. Each night I sing you a
fleet, Why should-n't we meet? When you're a - way from me

lov - er's song; Please try to hear, My dear, my dear.
days are sad; Life's not com - plete, My sweet, my sweet.

REFRAIN

Some-day I'll find you, Moon-light be-hind you, True to the dream I am dream - ing. As I draw near you You'll smile a lit-tle smile; For a lit-tle while We shall stand Hand in hand. I'll leave you

never, Love you for ev - er, All our past

sor - row re - deem - - ing: Try to make it true,

Say you love me too, Some-day I'll find you a - gain.

gain.

molto rall.

79

Mirabelle
[Lover of My Dreams]
from
CAVALCADE

(She) A sim-ple coun-try maid am I As in-no-cent as an-y flow - er; The great big world has pass'd me by, No lov-er comes my way to greet me shy - ly in my bow - er.

(He) Oh, say not so! Such mod-es-ty en-chants me:

Could I but stay to while a-way with you ____ a hap-py

hour. ___ (She) It must be Spring that fills my heart to ov-er-flow-ing.

Ah, whith-er am I go-ing? What is the voice that seems to say:

81

Be kind to love, don't let him call to you un - know - ing.

(He) If true love comes to you don't turn your face a - way.

(She) May-be 'tis some-thing in the air; For spring is made for lov-ers on - ly.

(He) Live for the mo-ment and take care, Lest love should fly and leave us lone - ly.

82

(Both) Ah, if love should leave us lone - ly.

REFRAIN

(She) All my life I have been wait - ing, Dream - ing a - ges through; _____ Un-til to-day I sud-den-ly dis-cov - -er The form and face of he who is my lov - er.

No more tears and hes - i - tat - ing, Fate has sent me you.____

____ ev - er, Time and tide can nev-er sev - er Those whom love has bound for-

- ev - er, Dear lov-er of my Dreams come true.

(He) All my life I have been wait - ing, Dream - ing a - ges

(She) All my life I have__ been wait - ing, Dream - ing a - ges

through;_____ Un-til to-day I sud-den-ly dis-

through;_____ Un-til to-day I sud-den-ly dis-

-cov - er, The form and face of she who is my

-cov - er, The form and face of he who is my

lov - er No more tears and hes-i-tat-ing,

lov - er No more tears and hes-i-tat-ing,

Fate has sent me you. _____ Time and tide can nev-er

Fate has sent me you._ Has sent_ me you and tide can nev-er

sev - er, Those whom love has bound for - ev - er, Dear lov-er of my

sev - er, Those whom love has bound for - ev - er, Dear lov-er of my

Dreams come true. _____

Dreams come true. _____

86

(Both) Dear lov-er of my Dreams come true,

Dear lov-er of my Dreams___ come true,_____

Dear lov-er of my Dreams___ come true._____

rall.

Twentieth Century Blues

from
CAVALCADE

Slow Blues Tempo

Why is it that civ-il-ised hu-man-i-ty can make this world so wrong?

In this hur-ly bur-ly of in-san-i-ty Our dreams can-not last long.

We've reach'd a dead-line, A press head-line ev - 'ry sor - row.

Blues va-lue is news va-lue to - mor - row.

REFRAIN

Blues, Twen-ti-eth Cen - tu-ry Blues — are get-ting me down.

Who's _____ es-cap'd those dreary

Twen-ti-eth Cen - tu-ry Blues? Why, if there's a god in the sky, ___ Why should-n't he grin High ___ ___ a-bove this dreary Twen-ti-eth Cen - tu-ry din? In this strange il-lu-sion, cha - os and con-fu-sion, Peo - ple seem to lose their way.

What is there to strive for, Love or keep a-live for? Say hey! hey!

call it a day!_ Blues, No-thing to win_ or to

lose,_ it's get-ting me down. Who's _____ es-cap'd those dreary

Twen-ti-eth Cen - tu-ry Blues? Blues?

Half Caste Woman

from
COCHRAN'S 1931 REVUE

Drink a bit, laugh a bit, love a bit more, I can sup-ply your need,

Think a bit, chaff a bit, what's it all for? That's my Eu - ra - sian creed.

Sail-ors with sen - ti - men-tal hearts who love and sail a - way,

When the dawn is grey Look at me and say—

REFRAIN

Half-caste woman, liv-ing a life a-part, Where did your sto-ry be-gin?

Half-caste woman, have you a se-cret heart Waiting for someone to win?

Were you born of some queer ma-gic In your shimmering gown?

93

Is there something strange and tra - gic Deep, deep down?

Half-caste woman, What are your slanting eyes Waiting and hoping to see?

Scanning the far ho - ri - zon Wondering what the end will be.

Down a-long the riv-er The sky is a-quiv-er, For

94

dawn is beginning to break;   Hear the syren's wailing, Some big ship is sailing And

losing my dreams in its wake.   Why should I remember the things that are past,

Moments so swift-ly gone;   Why wor-ry, for the Lord knows

time goes on.   Go to bed in daylight, Try to sleep in vain,

Get up in the ev-'ning, Work be-gins a-gain, Tin-ker, tai-lor, sol-dier, sai-lor,

rich man poor man, beggar man, thief, Questioning the same re - frain.

rall.

REFRAIN

Half-caste woman, living a life a-part, Where did your sto-ry be-gin?

Half-caste woman, have you a se-cret heart Waiting for someone to win?

sf

96

Were you born of some queer ma - gic In your shimmering gown?

Is there something strange and tra - gic Deep, deep down? Half-caste woman,

What are your slanting eyes Waiting and hoping to see Scanning the far ho - ri - zon,

Wondering what the end will be.

Any Little Fish

from

COCHRAN'S 1931 REVUE

I've fall-en in love with you

I'm tak-ing it bad - ly   Freez-ing, burn-ing, toss - ing, turn-ing

Nev-er know when to laugh or cry,   Just look what our dumb friends do

They wel-come it glad-ly. Pass-ion in a drom-e-da-ry does-n't go so deep, Cam-els when they're mat-ing nev-er sob them-selves to sleep, Buf-fa-los can rev-el in it, so can an-y sheep; Why can't I?

99

REFRAIN Quickly

An - y lit - tle fish can swim,
An - y lit - tle cock can crow,

An - y lit - tle bird can fly,
An - y lit - tle fox can run,

An - y lit - tle dog and an - y lit - tle cat Can
An - y lit - tle crab on an - y lit - tle shore Can

do a bit of this And just a bit of that;
have a lit - tle dab And then a lit - tle more;

An - y lit - tle horse can neigh,
An - y lit - tle owl can hoot, (To-whit To-whoo)

An - y lit - tle cow can moo,
An - y lit - tle dove can coo,

But I can't do an - y-thing at all But
But I can't do an - y-thing at all But

just love you.

just love you.

You've pulled me a-cross the brink, You've chained me and bound me, No es-cape now, buy the *crêpe* now, When is the fun -'ral going to be? When - ev-er I stop to think, See Na-ture all round me, Then I

see how stu-pid-ly mo-nog-a-mous I am, A lion, in the cir-cum-stan-ces

would-n't give a damn, For if there was no li-on-ess he'd

lie down with a lamb Why can't I?

REFRAIN Quickly

An-y lit-tle bug can bite,
An-y lit-tle duck can quack,

An-y lit-tle bee can buzz,
An-y lit-tle worm can crawl,

An-y lit-tle snail on an-y lit-tle oak Can feel a lit-tle frail and
An-y lit-tle mole can fro-lic in the sun And make a lit-tle hole And

have a lit-tle joke; An-y lit-tle frog can jump Like an-y lit-tle kan-ga-
have a lot of fun; An-y lit-tle snake can hiss In an-y lit-tle lo-cal

-roo, But I can't do an-y-thing at all But
Zoo, But I can't do an-y-thing at all But

just love you.
just love you.

I Travel Alone

Moderato

The world is wide, and when my day is done I shall at least have tra-vell'd

free, Led by this wan-der-lust That turns my eyes___ to far ho - ri - zons.

Though time and tide won't wait for an-y-one, There's one il-lu-sion left for me, And that's the hap-pi-ness I've known a-lone.

REFRAIN

I tra-vel a-lone. Sometimes I'm East, sometimes I'm West.

No chains can ev-er bind me; No remembered love can ev-er find me;

I tra-vel a - lone. Fair though the pla - ces and

fa-ces I've known, When the dream is end-ed and pas-sion has flown

I tra-vel a - lone. Free from love's il - lu-sion, my heart is my own;

I tra-vel a - lone. -lone.

rall.

sfz

106

Mrs. Worthington

Allegro moderato (*nice and breezy*)

Don't put your daugh-ter on the stage, Mis - sis Worth-ing-ton;

Don't put your daugh-ter on the stage._____ The pro -

-fes-sion is o - ver-crowd - ed and the strug-gle's pret - ty tough, And ad-

-mit-ting the fact, She's burn-ing to act, That is - n't quite e - nough. She has

nice hands, ___ to give the wretch-ed girl her due, But

don't you think her bust is too de - vel -oped for her age? I re-

-peat, Mis - sis Worth - ing-ton, Sweet Mis - sis Worth - ing-ton,

Don't put your daugh - ter on the stage.

VERSE

Re-gard-ing yours, dear Mis - sis Worth-ing-ton, Of Wed-nes-

-day the twen-ty - third; Al-though your ba - by May - be

109

Keen on a stage car-eer, How can I make it clear__ That this is not a good i-dea? For her to hope, Dear Mis-sis Worth-ing-ton, Is on the face of it ab-surd._____ Her per-son - al - i - ty Is not in re - al - i - ty In - vit-ing enough, Ex - cit-ing enough For this par-tic-u-lar sphere.

Don't put your daugh-ter on the stage, Mis - sis Worth-ing-ton;
Don't put your daugh-ter on the stage, Mis - sis Worth-ing-ton;

Don't put your daugh-ter on the stage. _____ She's a
Don't put your daugh-ter on the stage. _____ Tho' they

bit of an ug - ly duck-ling you must hon-est-ly con-fess, And the
said at the School of Act-ing she was love-ly as Peer Gynt I'm a-

width of her seat would sure-ly de-feat Her chan-ces of suc-cess. It's a
-fraid on the whole an in-gen-ue role Would em-pha-sise her squint. She's a

111

loud voice, and tho' it's not ex- act -ly flat She'll need a lit -tle
big girl and tho' her teeth are fair-ly good She's not the type I

more than that To earn a liv -ing wage. On my knees, Mis - sis
ev - er would Be eag -er to en - gage. No more buts, Mis - sis

Worth - ing-ton; Please, Mis - sis Worth - ing-ton, Don't put your
Worth - ing-ton; NUTS, Mis - sis Worth - ing-ton, Don't put your

daughter on the stage.
daughter on the stage.

112

Mad Dogs and Englishmen

from
WORDS AND MUSIC

INTRO.
Briskly

1. In trop-i-cal climes there are cer-tain times of day _____
2. It's such a sur-prise for the East-ern eyes to see, _____

_When all the cit-i-zens re-tire To tear their
_That though the Eng-lish are ef-fete, They're quite im-

clothes off and per - spire. It's one of those rules that the great - est fools o -
-per - vi - ous to heat. When the white man rides ev - 'ry na - tive hides in

-bey,_____ Be - cause the sun is much too sul - try And one
glee._____ Be - cause the sim - ple crea - tures hope he Will im -

must a - void its ul - try - vio - let ray.
-pale his so - lar to - pee on a tree.

CHORUS

Pa - pa - la - ka pa - pa - la - ka
Bo - ly - bo - ly bo - ly - bo - ly

pa - pa - la - ka boo, Pa - pa - la - ka pa - pa - la - ka pa - pa - la - ka boo,
bo - ly - bo - ly baa, Bo - ly - bo - ly bo - ly - bo - ly bo - ly - bo - ly baa,

Di - ga - ri - ga di - ga - ri - ga di - ga - ri - ga doo,
Ha - ba - nin - ny ha - ba - nin - ny ha - ba - nin - ny haa,

Di - ga - ri - ga di - ga - ri - ga di - ga - ri - ga doo. The
Ha - ba - nin - ny ha - ba - nin - ny ha - ba - nin - ny haa. It

SOLO

na - tives grieve when the white men leave their huts, Be - cause they're
seems such a shame when the Eng - lish claim the earth That they give

ob - vi - ous - ly de - fin - ite - ly Nuts!
rise to such hi - lar - i - ty and mirth.

115

REFRAIN

116

glare. In the Ma - lay States there are hats like plates Which the Bri - tish - ers won't
beast The Eng-lish garb of the Eng - lish Sa-hib Mere-ly gets a bit more

two. Ev-en ca - ri - bous lie a - round and snooze, For there's no-thing else to

wear. At twelve noon the na - tives swoon And no fur-ther work is
creased. In Bang - kok at twelve o' - clock They foam at the mouth and
do. In Ben - gal, to move at all Is sel - dom, if ev - er

done. But mad dogs and Eng-lish-men Go
run. But mad dogs and Eng-lish-men Go
done. But mad dogs and Eng-lish-men Go

1 & 2 · **3**

out in the mid-day sun.——
out in the mid-day sun.——
out in the mid-day sun.——

fz

Mad about the Boy

from

WORDS AND MUSIC

I met him at a par-ty just a cou-ple of years a-go, He was ra-ther o-ver heart-y, and ri-dic-u-lous,___ But as I'd

118

seen him on the Screen He cast a cer - tain spell.

I bask'd in his at-trac-tion for a cou-ple of hours or so,___ His

man-ners were a frac-tion too met - i - cu -lous. ___ If he was real or not I could - n't

tell, But like a sil - ly fool, I fell.

REFRAIN

Mad a-bout the boy,____ I know it's stu-pid to be mad a-bout the boy,____ I'm so a-shamed of it But must ad-mit The sleep-less nights I've had a-bout the boy.

On the Sil-ver Screen____ He melts my fool-ish heart in ev-'ry sin-gle scene,____ Al-though I'm quite a-ware That here and there Are tra-ces of the cad a-bout the boy.

Lord knows I'm not a fool girl, I real-ly should-n't care,

Lord knows I'm not a school girl, In the flur-ry of her first af - fair.

Will it ev-er cloy?___ This odd di-ver-si-ty of mis-er-y and joy___ I'm feel-ing

quite in-sane And young a-gain And all be-cause I'm mad a-bout the boy.___

It seems a lit-tle sil-ly For a girl of my age and weight To walk down Pic-ca-dil-ly In a haze of love __ It ought to take a good deal more to get a bad girl down, I should have been ex-empt, for My par-ti-cu-lar kind of Fate __ Has

taught me such con-tempt for Ev-'ry phase of love,— And now I've been and spent my last half-

-crown To weep a-bout a paint-ed clown.

REFRAIN

Mad a-bout the boy,— It's pret-ty fun-ny but I'm mad a-bout the boy.— He has a

gay ap-peal That makes me feel There's may-be some-thing sad a-bout the boy.

Walk-ing down the street,____ His eyes look out at me from peo-ple that I meet;____

____ I can't be-lieve it's true, But when I'm blue, In some strange way I'm

glad a-bout the boy.   I'm hard-ly sen-i-men-tal,

Love is-n't so sub-lime,   I have to pay my

rent - al And I can't af - ford to waste much time,

If I could em - ploy___ A lit - tle ma - gic that would fin - al - ly des - troy___

___ This dream that pains me And enchains me, But I can't, be - cause I'm mad a - bout the boy.

rall.

125

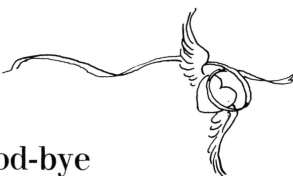

Let's Say Good-bye

from

WORDS AND MUSIC

Now we've em - bark'd on this love af - fair, Don't let's des -

-troy it with tears, _____ Once we be - gin to let

sen - ti - ment in, Hap - pi - ness dis - ap - pears. ____

Rea - son may sleep for a mo - ment in spring, But please let us

keep this a cas - u - al thing, Some - thing that's sweet to re -

- mem - ber through the years. ____

REFRAIN

Let our af - fair be a gay thing,_____

And when these hours__ have flown._____

Then, with - out for - get - ting Hap - pi - ness that has passed,

There'll be no re - gret - ting Fun that did - n't quite last.

128

Let's look on love as a play - thing,_____ All these sweet mo-ments we've known_____ Must - n't be de-grad-ed When the thrill of them has fad - ed, Let's say 'Good - bye' and leave it a - lone._____

The Party's Over Now

from

WORDS AND MUSIC

Night is o-ver, dawn is break-ing, Ev-'ry-where the Town is wak-ing,

Just as we are on our way to sleep.

Lov-ers meet and dance a lit-tle, Snatch-ing from ro-mance a lit-tle Sou-ve-nir of hap-pi-ness to keep._____ The mu-sic of an hour a-go_____ Was just a sort of Let's pre-tend, The mel-o-dies that charmed us so_____ At last are end - ed._____ The

131

REFRAIN

Par - ty's o - ver now, The dawn is draw-ing ve - ry nigh, ___ The can-dles gut - ter, the star-light leaves the sky, ___ It's time for lit - tle boys and girls To hur - ry home to bed, ___ For there's a new day wait-ing just a- -head. ___ Life is sweet But time is fleet, Be-neath the

mag - ic of the moon Danc - ing time May seem sub-lime, But it is end - ed all too

soon._____ The thrill has gone, To ling - er on Would spoil it a - ny-how:_____

_Let's creep a - way from the day For the par - ty's o - ver

1
now.

2
The now._____

8va

pp

I'll Follow
My Secret Heart

from
CONVERSATION PIECE

SPOKEN. *(Melanie)* When may I love somebody, please?

(Paul) Not until you are safely married and then only with greatest discretion.

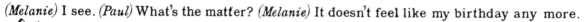

(Melanie) I see. *(Paul)* What's the matter? *(Melanie)* It doesn't feel like my birthday any more.

A cloud has pass'd a-cross the sun _____ The morning seems no long-er

gay.

With so much bus'ness to be

done_____ Ev-en the sea looks grey C'est vrai! C'est

vrai! It seems that all the joy has fad-ed for the day_____ As though the

fool-ish world no long-er wants to play.

You ask me to have a dis-creet heart Un-til

mar-riage is out of the way But what if I meet with a

sweet - heart so sweet That my wayward heart___ can-not o - bey___

A sin-gle word that you may say?   Then we shall have to go a-

-way.   No

___ for there is nowhere we could go ___ Where we could hide from what we

know   Is   true.

Don't be a-fraid I'll be-tray you And des-troy all the plans you have made, But

ev - en your schemes must leave room for my dreams, So when all I owe___ to you is paid

I'll still have something of my own, A lit-tle prize that's mine a - lone.

I'll fol-low my se - cret heart my whole life through,___

138

I'll keep all my dreams a-part till one comes true___

___ No mat-ter what price is paid, What stars may fade a-

-bove___ I'll fol-low my se-cret heart till I

find love.___ love.___

rall.

Ped. ✳

139

Nevermore

from

CONVERSATION PIECE

Moderato

Dear friend, If hearts could on - ly be Con - tent with love and sym - pa - thy, How sweet - ly we could live! We

both of us have so much love to give._____ No mat-ter how our minds con-spire, Im - pris-on'd by our own de-sire We are not free to choose What love we gain What love we lose,_____ We can-not choose.

ten.

141

REFRAIN *Nice and flowing*

Nev - er - more, Nev - er - more, Can life be quite the same. _____ The lights and sha - dows change, _____ All the old fam - i - liar world is strange _____ Ev - er - more, Ev - er -

142

-more   Our   hearts   are   in   the   flame,_____

Oth - ers   may   re - gain   their   free - dom   But   for   you   and

me   Nev - er,   Nev - er - more.

-more._____

143

Regency Rakes

from

CONVERSATION PIECE

Valse tempo

f

You may think, _____ Look-ing at the four of us, Food and drink _____ Con-sti-tute the core of us. That may be, But still you'll see Our

names on pos - ter - i - ty's page._____ You will read _____ His - tor - ies ga - lore of us, Strut - ting Eng - land's stage _____ We re - pre - sent To a cer - tain ex - -tent The in - ef - fa - ble scent Of our Age._____ We're

REFRAIN

Re-gen-cy Rakes, And each of us takes A per-son-al pride In the
Re-gen-cy Rakes, And each of us makes A per-son-al is-sue Of

thick-ness of hide Which pre-vents us from see-ing How vul-gar we're be-ing With-
ad-i-pose tis-sue. But still not-with-stand-ing Our stomachs ex-pand-ing, We

-out mak-ing us wince._____ We're ruth-less and rude And
all yearn for ro-mance._____ We fre-quent-ly start Af-

boast of a crude And lord-ly dis-dain Both for mind and for brain; Tho' ob-
-fairs of the heart, Su-blime-ly un-heed-ing That long ov-er-feed-ing Has

-tuse and slow - wit - ted We're not to be pit - ied For we fol - low the
made so dis - gust - ing Our lov - ing or lust - ing That girls eye us as -

Prince._____ Ev - 'ry or - gy With our Geor - gie Lasts 'till
-kance._____ Tho' we won - der, As we blun - der In - to

dawn with - out a lull;_____ We can ven - ture With - out
this or that bor - del,_____ Whom we know there, Why we

cen - sure To be noi - sy, drunk, and dull!_____ We
go there, But we're far too drunk to tell._____ Tho'

147

rev-el in Sport, Ma-dei-ra, and Port, And when we pass out With scle-
ov-er-jo-cose, Un-fun-ny and gross, We don't lose a frac-tion Of

-ro-sis and gout All our chil-dren will rue our mis-takes, _____
self-sat-is-fac-tion. Com-pla-cen-cy nev-er for-sakes _____

Roy-ster-ing Re-gen-cy Rakes, _____ Roy-ster-ing
Roy-ster-ing Re-gen-cy Rakes, _____ Roy-ster-ing

Re-gen-cy Rakes. We're
Re-gen-cy Rakes. _____

We Were Dancing

from

TONIGHT AT EIGHT-THIRTY

If you can——— i - ma-gine my em - bar-rass-ment when you po -

-lite - ly ask me to ex - plain man to ·man——— I can-not help but

feel con - ven - tion - al a - pol - o - gies are all in vain. You must see___

___we've stepped in - to a dream That's set us free, Don't think we

planned it, Please un - der - stand it.

REFRAIN

We were danc - ing___ and the Gods must have found it en -

mf rall.   *a tempo*

150

-tranc - ing___ For they smiled ___ on a mo - ment ___

_ un - de - filed _____ By the care and woe that

mor - tals know, We were danc - ing ___ And the mu - sic and

lights were en - hanc - ing ___ our de - sire _____ When the

world_____ caught on fire_____ She and I were danc-ing.

Love lay in wait for us,

Twist-ed our fate for us, No one warned us, Rea - son

scorned us. Time stood still_____ In that

152

first　　　　strange　　　　thrill.　　　　　　　　　　　　Des - ti - ny

knew of us Guid - ed the two of us How could we re -

-fuse to　　see　that　wrong　　　seemed　　　right On this

ly - ric - al en - chant - ed　　　night.

153

Log-ic sup-plies no laws for it, On-ly one

cause for it.   We were

REFRAIN

danc-ing___ And the Gods must have found it en-tranc-ing___ For they

smiled_____ on a mo-ment un-de-filed_____ By the

154

care and woe that mor - tals know. We were danc - ing

And the mu - sic and lights were en - hanc - ing our de -

-sire When the world caught on fire

She and I were danc-ing.

You Were There

from

SHADOW PLAY

1. Was___ it in the real world? Or was___ it in a
2. How___ could we ex-plain it, The spark___ and then the

dream? Was___ it just a note___ in some e-
fire? How___ add up the to - tal of our

-ter - nal theme. Was___ it ac - ci - den - tal Or
heart's de - sire? May - be some ma - gi - cian A

ac - cur - ate - ly planned? How could I hes - i -
thou - sand years a - go Wove us a sub - tle

-tate Know-ing that my fate Led me by the hand.
spell So that we could tell, So that we could know.

rall.

REFRAIN
Nice and lightly

You were there I saw you and my heart stopped beat-ing

mp-f

You were there, And in that first en-chant-ed meet-ing

Life changed its tune, the stars and moon came near to me.

Dreams that I dreamed, like mag-ic seemed to be clear to me, Dear to me,

rall.

You were there, Your eyes looked in-to mine and falt-ered

Ev - ery - where   the co - lour of the whole world al - tered

False be - came true My u - ni - verse tum - bled in two The earth be - came

hea - ven for You __ were there.

1

2

there.

rall.

159

Play, Orchestra, Play!

from

SHADOW PLAY

Allegro moderato

Lis-ten to the strain   it plays once more for us

There it is a - gain____ The past in

store for us.   Wake____ in mem-o-ry some for-got-ten song to

160

break _____ the rhy-thm Driv-ing us a-long and make

Har-mo-ny a-gain _____ a last en-core for us.

REFRAIN

Play, or - ches - tra, play, _____ Play some-thing

light and sweet and gay _____ For we

must have mu-sic, we must have mu-sic To drive _____ our

fears a - way, _ While our il - lu - sions swift - ly fade _ for us

Let's have an or-ches-tra score. _____ In the con - fu-sions the

years have made _ for us Ser - en - ade _ for us just once

162

more Life need-n't be grey_____ al-though it's chang-ing

day by day_____ Tho' a few old dreams may de-

-cay_____ Play, or-ches-tra, Play!

Play!

163

Dearest Love

from

OPERETTE

Allegro moderato

pp

mp

I saw your face   Shadows of the morning cleared,   I knew that sud-den-ly the

world had dropp'd a-way.   Somewhere in space   Some new love-ly star appeared

To rule our des-ti - ny For ev- er and a day. I knew, the mo-ment that I

touched your hand, The Gods had planned Our meet - ing.

Now in this in-stant in the whole of Time Our lov - er's rhyme Is near com-

-plet - ing. I saw you turn a-way and for a while my

poco rall.

accel.

165

poor heart drooped and fal-tered; And then I saw your strange e-

-lu-sive smile And all my life was al-tered My dearest dear

For ev-er-more The hap-pi-ness we've wait-ed for At last is here

rall - en - tan - do

REFRAIN Valse moderato

Dear - est love, Now that I've found you The stars change in the sky,

mp

166

Every song is new ____ Every note is true ____ Sorrows like the clouds go

sail - ing by. ____ Here my love, Mag-ic has bound you to

me - ev- er to be ____ In my heart su - preme, Dearer than my

dear - est dream, The on - ly love for me. ____

Skies that were cloud-y are clear a-gain,_ All oth-er peo-ple seem_ _ Like figures in a dream;_ Ev-'ry song that I loved I seem to hear a-gain,_ Time goes by like a mur-mur-ing stream._ Love has en-chant-ed the two of us,_ A mag-ic we can share,_

168

A something in the air, _____ Prov - ing that Des - ti - ny

knew of us _____ Now Heav'n is at our feet, _____ This hap - pi - ness com - plete_____

_Could not be merely chance; _____ This ex - quis - ite ro - mance _____ For ev - er has us

bound, For this that we have found No time or tide could sev - er ev - er.

poco rall.

rall.

169

Dear - est love, Now that I've found you The
stars change in the sky, _____ Ev -'ry song is
new, _____ Ev -'ry note is true, _____ Sor-rows like the
clouds go sail - ing by. _____

a tempo

170

Here my love, Mag - ic has bound you To me ev - er to be _____ In my heart su - preme, _____ Dear-er than my dear - est dream, The on - ly love for me! _____

rall.

171

Where are the Songs We Sung?

from
OPERETTE

This is the on - ly and the last time.
That pass - ing years have o - ver - tak - en?

That young sur - ren - der
Youth is be - hind us

We can re - mem - ber when some lit - tle tune
We can - not live a - mong our yes - ter - days

Re - calls our hearts to van - ished splen - dour
Nor let their light for - ev - er blind us

173

Like or - gan mu - sic in a sun - ny street
For with the wis - dom of our lat - er days

So sweet - ly flat, so sad - ly ten - der.
Per - haps some deep - er love may find us

And so when love a - gain rides
But still tho' life may make us

by We some - times sigh
wise An e - cho cries

rall.

REFRAIN Valse moderato

Where are the songs we sung
Where are the songs we sung

When love in our hearts was young? Where, in the
When love in our hearts was young? Can you re-

lim-bo of the swift-ly pass - ing years, Lie all our
-mem-ber all the fool-ish things we said, The plans we

hopes and dreams and fears? Where have they gone —
planned — the tears we shed? Where is it now —

words that rang so true   When   love in our
that en - chant - ed dawn   When   love in our

hearts was new?   Where, in the   sha-dows that we have to pass a -
hearts was born?   Where, in the   sha-dows that we have to pass a -

-mong,   Lie those songs that once we sung?
-mong,   Lie those songs that once we

1

2

sung?

rall.

176

The Stately Homes of England

from

OPERETTE

Lord El - der-ley, Lord Bor-row-mere, Lord Sick-ert And Lord Camp— With ev-'ry vir-tue, ev-'ry grace, Are what a-vails the sceptred race.

Copyright MCMXXXVIII by Chappell & Co. Ltd.

Here you see _____ the four of us, And there are so ma-ny more of us
Here you see _____ The pick of us You may be heart-i - ly sick of us

Eld - est sons _____ that must suc - ceed, _____ We know how
Still with sense _____ We're all im - bued _____ Our homes com-

Cae - sar con-quer'd Gaul And how to whack a cric - ket ball, A - part from
-mand ex - ten - sive views. And with as - sist - ance from the Jews. We have been

this, our ed - u - ca - tion Lacks co - or - di - na - tion.
a - ble to dis - pose of Rows and rows and rows of

L.H.

178

Tho' we're young ___ and ten-ta-tive And rath-er rip-re-pre-sent-a-tive,
Gains-bor-oughs ___ and Lawrences Some sport-ing prints of Aunt Flor-en-ce's

Sci-ons of ___ a no-ble breed, ___ We are the
Some of which ___ were rath-er rude ___ Al-tho' we

pro-ducts of those homes ser-ene and state-ly ___ Which on-ly
some-times flaunt our fam-i-ly con-ven-tions ___ Our good in-

late-ly ___ Seem to have run to seed! ___ The
-ten-tions ___ Must-n't be mis-con-strued. ___ The

rall.

179

REFRAIN

Stately Homes of England How beautiful they stand,—— To
prove the upper classes Have still the upper hand; Tho' the
fact that they have to be re-built And frequently mortgag'd to the hilt Is in-
-clin'd to take the gilt —————— Off the ginger-bread, And certainly damps the

Stately Homes of England We proudly represent,—— We
only keep them up for Americans to rent. Tho' the
pipes that supply the bath-room burst And the lav-a-t'ry makes you fear the worst It was
used by Charles the First —————— Quite informally, And later by George the

fun   Of the eld-est son ___ But still we won't be beat-en, We'll
Fourth   On a jour-ney North, __ The State A-part-ments keep their His-

scrimp and screw and save, __ The play-ing fields of E - ton Have made us fright-fully
-to - ri -cal re - nown,- It's wi - ser not to sleep there In case they tum-ble

brave___ And tho' if the Van Dycks have to go And we pawn the Bechstein Grand, We'll
down;_ But still if they ev - er catch on fire Which with an - y luck, they might, We'll

stand by the State - ly Homes of Eng - land.___
fight for the State - ly Homes of Eng - land._____ The

fz

3rd REFRAIN

State - ly Homes of Eng - land, Tho' rath - er in the lurch,— Pro - vide a lot of chanc - es For Psy - chi - cal Re - search—There's the ghost of a cra - zy young - er son Who mur - der'd in Thir - teen Fif - ty - One, An ex - treme - ly row - dy Nun ____ Who re - sent - ed it, And peo - ple who come to call Meet her in the

182

hall. _ The ba-by in the guest wing Who crouch-es by the grate, _ Was

wall'd up in the west wing In Four-teen Twen-ty - Eight. _ If a - ny-one spots The

Queen of Scots In a hand em-broid-er'd shroud, We're

proud of the State-ly Homes of Eng - land. _

Never Again
from
SET TO MUSIC

O - ver now,____ The dream is o - ver now,____
____May-be it real-ly was-n't so im - por - tant a - ny how.____ What's been can't
be a - gain. Re-luc-tant - ly I see,____ My heart is free a - gain,____

Be-longs to me a-gain.___ The brief il - lu - sion I lived for has

gone._____ No more con - fu - sion and tears from now

on;_____ To start a-gain___ And break my heart a-gain_

_ If you should ask me to,___ I'd say, {"To hell with you!"___
"A - way with you!"___

185

REFRAIN (*slowly with expression*)

No,_____ nev-er a-gain,_____ Nev-er the strange un-think-ing joy, Nev-er the pain; Let me be wise,_____ Let me learn to doubt ro-mance,___ Try to live with-out ro-mance,___ Let me be sane._____ Time_____

chan-ges the tune;_____ Chan-ges the pale un-wink-ing

stars, Ev-en the moon._____ Let me be soon _____ Strong e-nough to

flout ro - mance __ And say "You're out, ro - mance," __ Nev-er a - gain! _____

-gain! _____

I Went to a Marvellous Party

from

ALL CLEAR

Ev-'ry one's here and fright-f'lly gay, No-bod-y cares what peo - ple say,

Tho' the Ri-vie-ra Seems real-'ly much queer-er Than Rome at its height. Yes-ter-day night.

REFRAIN
p-mf

I went to a mar-vel-lous par - ty___ I must say the fun was in-

-tense, ___ We all had to do what the peo-ple we knew Would be

do-ing a hun-dred years hence.____ Dear Ce-cil ar-rived wear-ing

ar-mour_ Some shells and a black feath-er boa.__ Poor Mill-i-cent wore a sur-

-re-al-ist comb Made of bits of Mo-saic from St. Pe-ter's in Rome, But the

weight was so great that she had to go home, I

could'-nt have liked it more!_ I more!_

The Forties

'London Pride' was written in the spring of 1941. I was standing on the platform of a London railway station on the morning after a bad blitz. Most of the glass in the station roof had been blown out and there was dust in the air and the smell of burning. The train I was waiting to meet was running late and so I sat on a platform seat and watched the Londoners scurrying about in the thin spring sunshine. They all seemed to me to be gay and determined and wholly admirable and for a moment or two I was overwhelmed by a wave of sentimental pride. The song started in my head then and there and was finished in a couple of days. The tune is based on the old traditional lavender-seller's song 'Won't you buy my sweet blooming lavender, there are sixteen blue bunches one penny'. This age-old melody was appropriated by the Germans and used as a foundation for 'Deutschland über Alles', and I considered that the time had come for us to have it back in London where it belonged.

I am proud of the words of this song. They express what I felt at the time and what I still feel, i.e. London Pride.

'Could You please oblige us with a Bren Gun?' was too topical to outlive for long its immediate moment. I think, however, that it has some funny lines in it and as a period piece is not without merit.

191

There Have Been Songs in England

★

Don't Let's Be Beastly to the Germans

'There Have Been Songs in England' is quite pleasant but, to my mind, a little pretentious. It is heavy and soggy and fares ill in comparison with 'London Pride'. 'Don't Let's Be Beastly to the Germans' I think is a very good satirical song indeed. It was also, quite unwittingly, scathingly prophetic. When it was first written in the spring of 1943 Mr. Winston Churchill liked it so much that I had to sing it to him seven times in one evening. On the other hand, certain rather obtuse members of the general public objected to it on the grounds that it was pro-German! This odd misconception flung both the B.B.C. and His Master's Voice Gramophone Company into a panic. The former organization refused to allow it to be broadcast and the latter suppressed for three months the record I had made of it. I was away at the time, entertaining troops in the Middle East, and knew nothing of this rumpus until my return. Later on, the song became absorbed into the public consciousness in its correct perspective and now 'Don't let's be beastly . . .' has become a catch phrase. I shall never cease to be surprised at the sublime silliness of some of those protesting letters. After all, 'Let's help the dirty swine again to occupy the Rhine again' and 'Let's give them full air-parity and treat the rats with charity' are not, as phrases, exactly oozing with brotherly love. International circumstances have by now set the seal of irony on the whole thing. I must really be more careful what I write about in future.

This is the End of the News

★

Nina

★

I Wonder What Happened to Him

These five numbers were all in 'Sigh No More', a revue produced at the Piccadilly Theatre in the autumn of 1945. They were, however, written at different times and in different places. 'This is the End of the News', for instance, was begun and completed in H.M.S. *Charybdis*, a light cruiser in which I was given passage to Gibraltar in 1943. 'Nina' was begun in Pietermaritzburg in South Africa and finished in a train between Bloemfontein and Pretoria.

'I Wonder What Happened to Him' was written and firmly sung in Calcutta in 1944. Only a very few outraged 'Indian Colonels' protested and it was a great success.

Matelot

Sigh No More

★

Matelot

'Sigh No More' was the opening number of the revue and musically I am very attached to it in spite of the fact that it is a devil to sing.

'Matelot', in my opinion, is one of the best songs I ever wrote. The words are staunchly married to the music and the whole has charm and atmosphere. It was beautifully sung by Graham Payn and it has remained strongly embedded in my affections to this day.

This is a Changing World

★

His Excellency Regrets

★

Bright Was The Day

These three songs are from the score of 'Pacific 1860,' produced in 1946. 'This is a Changing World' was sung exquisitely by Sylvia Cecil in the second act. 'His Excellency Regrets' was a double sextette performed with considerable verve by twelve attractive young people whose enthusiasm compensated, up to a point, for their lack of diction. 'Bright Was The Day' was the principal waltz song, sung by Mary Martin and Graham Payn. It has a nice melodic refrain, but from the musical and lyrical point of view I prefer the verse.

London Pride

Moderato (*Not too slowly*)

1. Lon-don Pride has been handed down to us.
2. Lon-don Pride has been handed down to us.

Lon-don Pride is a flow-er that's free. Lon-don Pride means our own dear town to us,
Lon-don Pride is a flow-er that's free. Lon-don Pride means our own dear town to us,

And our pride it for ev-er will be. Woa Li-za see the cos-ter bar-rows,
And our pride it for ev-er will be. Hey la-dy when the day is dawn-ing

Veg - e - ta - ble mar-rows and the fruit piled high. Woa Li - za
See the p'liceman yawn-ing on his lone - ly beat. Gay la - dy

lit - tle Lon-don spar-rows, Cov-ent Gar - den Mar-ket where the cos - ters cry.
May-fair in the morn-ing. Hear the foot-steps ech - o in the emp - ty street.

poco rall.

Cock-ney feet mark the beat of his - to - ry. Ev - 'ry street pins a mem - o - ry down.
Ear - ly rain and the pavements glist-en-ing. All Park Lane in a shimmer-ing gown.

a tempo

Noth-ing ev - er can quite re-place The grace of Lon - don Town.
Noth-ing ev - er could break or harm The charm of Lon - don Town.

poco rall.

196

INTERLUDE

There's a lit-tle ci-ty flow'r- ev-'ry spring un-fail-ing Growing in the cre-vi-ces
In our ci-ty darkened now- street and squares and crescent We can feel our liv-ing past

by some Lon-don rail-ing Tho' it has a Lat-in name, in
in our sha-dowed pre - sent Ghosts be-side our star-lit Thames who

town and coun-try-side We in Eng-land call it Lon-don Pride.
lived and loved and died Keep throughout the a - ges Lon-don Pride.

poco rall.

D. %

Lon-don Pride has been hand-ed down to us. Lon-don Pride is a flow-er that's free.

197

Lon-don Pride means our own dear town to us, And our pride it for ev-er will be.

mf gaily

Grey ci-ty stub-born-ly im-plant-ed, Tak-en so for granted for a thou-sand years.

Stay ci-ty smok-i-ly en-chant-ed, Cra-dle of our mem-o-ries and hopes and fears.

poco rall.

a tempo

Ev-'ry Blitz your re-sist-ance tough-en-ing From the Ritz to the Anch-or and Crown,

Noth-ing ev-er could ov-er-ride The pride of Lon-don Town.

rall. *fz*

Could You Please Oblige Us with a Bren Gun?

Tempo di Marcia

1. Colo - nel Mont-mor - en - cy who Was in Cal-cut -ta in nine - ty two E-
2. Colo - nel Mont-mor - en - cy planned In case the en-e-my tried to land To

-merged from his re - tire - ment for the war. He
fling them back by skill and arm - oured force. He

was-n't ve - ry pleased with what he heard and what he saw. ____ What-
re - a-lised his ar - my should be me - chan-ised, of course; ___ But

- ev - er he felt He tight-ened his belt And or - gan-ised a corps- poor
somewhere in-side Ex - pe - ri - ence cried:"My king-dom for a horse" poor

Colo - nel Mont-mor - en - cy thought,Con-sid-er-ing all the wars he'd fought,The
Colo - nel Mont-mor - en - cy tried At in-fin-ite cost of time and pride To

Home Guard was his job to do or die; _____ But
tac - kle his su - pe - ri - ors a - gain _____ To

af - ter days and weeks and years Brave-ly dry-ing his man-ly tears He
Hav-ing just one mo-tor-bike, Four-teen swords and a mar-lin-spike, He

wrote the fol-low-ing let - ter to the Min-is-ter of Sup-ply.___
couched the fol-low-ing let - ter in the fol-low-ing ur-gent strain.___

REFRAIN

1. Could you please o - blige us with a Bren gun?___ Or
2. Could you please o - blige us with a Bren gun?___ We're
3. Could you please o - blige us with a Bren gun?___ We
4. Could you please o - blige us with a Bren gun?___ The

fail - ing that a hand.-gren-ade would do.___ We've
get - ting aw - fully tired of draw-ing lots.___ To -
need it ra - ther bad - ly I'm a - fraid.___ Our
lack of one is wound - ing to our pride.___ Last

201

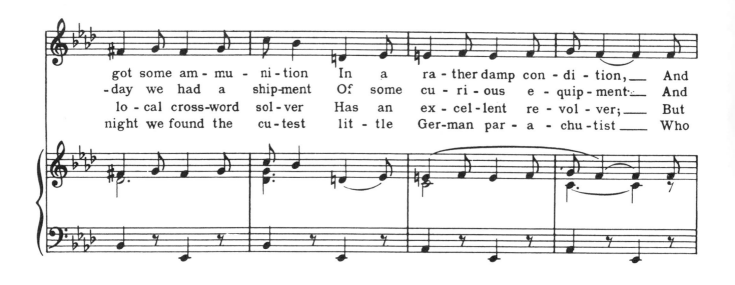

got some am - mu - ni - tion In a ra - ther damp con - di - tion,___ And
-day we had a ship-ment Of some cu - ri - ous e - quip-ment___ And
lo - cal cross-word sol - ver Has an ex - cel - lent re - vol - ver;___ But
night we found the cu - test lit - tle Ger-man par - a - chu-tist___ Who

Ma - jor Huss has an Ar - que-bus that was used at Wa - ter - loo.
just for a prank they sent us a tank that ties it - self in knots.___ On
dur - ing a short at - tack on a fort the trig - ger got mis-laid.___ In
look'd at our kit and gig-gled a bit, then laugh'd un - til he cried.___ We'll

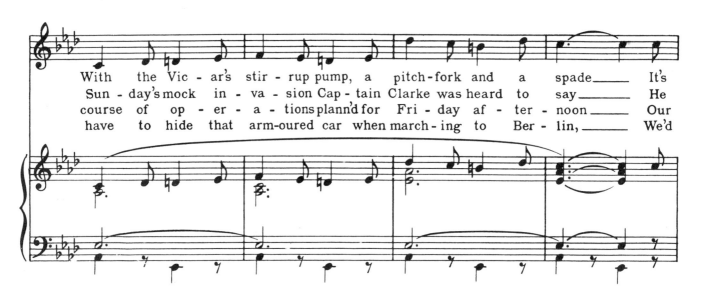

With the Vic - ar's stir - rup pump, a pitch-fork and a spade___ It's
Sun - day's mock in - va - sion Cap - tain Clarke was heard to say___ He
course of op - er - a - tions plann'd for Fri - day af - ter - noon___ Our
have to hide that arm-oured car when march-ing to Ber - lin,___ We'd

ra - ther hard to guard an aer - o - drome; _____ So if you can't o-
had - n't ev - en got a brush and comb; _____ So if you can't o-
or - ders are to storm the Hip - po - drome; _____ So if you can't o-
al - most be a - shamed of it in Rome. _____ So if you can't o-

-blige us with a Bren gun __ The Home Guard might as well go
-blige us with a Bren gun __ The Home Guard might as well go
-blige us with a Bren gun __ The Home Guard might as well go
-blige us with a Bren gun __ The Home Guard might as well go

home. _____   home. _____
home. _____   home. _____
home. _____   home. _____
home. _____   home. _____

There have been Songs in England

Moderato (*In a flowing manner*)

A na-tion's mu-sic be-longs to the Race Thro' the slow time chan-ges and the rhy-thm of moving years. Our na-tion's songs are its pride and its grace Ev-er-more and af-ter Tho' the

mf *poco rit.* *p a tempo*

shape of the world may al - ter In our songs the laugh-ter Blends the

tears. From the past _____ we hear the ec - ho of the

songs that proved us free They are be-queath'd to

poco rit.

you and me for ev - er and ev - er.

poco rit.

REFRAIN

There have been songs in Eng - land ____ Since our is - land rose from the seas ____ As the dry land lay on that ear-ly English day A sea - wind rus-tled thro' the trees ____ Ve - ry soon the birds ap-pear'd La - ter, ly-ric words ap-pear'd La - ter on the peo-ple sang

Still they're sing-ing free. There have been songs in Eng -

- land And songs there will al - ways be. al - ways

be. There have been songs in Eng - land And

songs there will al - ways be.

Don't Let's Be Beastly to the Germans

Moderato

1. We must be
2. We must be

kind
just

And with an o - pen mind
And win their love and trust

We must en - dea-vour to find a
And in add - i - tion we must be

way _____
wise _____

To let the Ger-mans know that when the war is o - ver
And ask the conquered lands to join our hands to aid them

They are not the ones who'll have to pay⎯
That would be a won-der-ful sur-prise⎯

We must be sweet
For ma-ny years

And tact-ful and dis-creet
They've been in floods of tears

And when they've suffer'd de-feat We must-n't let them
Because the poor lit-tle dears Have been so wrong'd and

feel up-set Or ev-er get the feel-ing that we're cross with them or
on-ly long'd To cheat the world, de-plete the world and beat the world to

hate them. Our fu-ture pol-i-cy must be to re-in-state them.
blaz-es This is the mo-ment when we ought to sing their prais-es.

REFRAIN

1. Don't let's be beast-ly to the Ger-mans_____ When our Vic-tor-y is
2. Don't let's be beast-ly to the Ger-mans_____ When we've de-fin-ite-ly
3. Don't let's be beast-ly to the Ger-mans_____ When the age of peace and
4. Don't let's be beast-ly to the Ger-mans_____ For you can't de-prive a

ul-ti-mate-ly won_____ It was just those nas-ty Naz-is who per-
got them on the run_____ Let us treat them ve-ry kind-ly as we
plen-ty has be-gun_____ We must send them steel and oil and coal and
gang-ster of his gun_____ Tho'they've been a lit-tle naugh-ty to the

-suad-ed them to fight_____ And their Beet-ho-ven and Bach are real-ly
would a val-ued friend_____ We might send them out some Bish-ops as a
ev-'ry-thing they need_____ For their peace-a-ble in-ten-tions can be
Czechs and Poles and Dutch_____ But I don't sup-pose those coun-tries real-ly

far worse than their bite   Let's_____ be meek to them And turn the oth-er
form of lease and lend   Let's_____ be sweet to them And day by day re-
al-ways guar-an-teed   Let's_____ em-ploy with them A sort of strength thro'
mind-ed ve-ry much   Let's_____ be free with them And share the B. B.

210

cheek to them And try to bring out their la - tent sense of fun_____
-peat to them That 'ster - i - li - za - tion' sim - ply is - n't done._____
joy' with them They're bet - ter than us at hon - est man - ly fun_____
C. with them We must - n't pre - vent them bask - ing in the sun_____

_____ Let's give them full air par - i - ty And treat the rats with
_____ Let's help the dir - ty swine a - gain To oc - cu - py the
_____ Let's let them feel they're swell a - gain And bomb us all to
_____ Let's soft - en their de - feat a - gain And build their blood - y

char - i - ty But don't let's be beast - ly to the Hun._____
Rhine a - gain But don't let's be beast - ly to the Hun._____
hell a - gain But don't let's be beast - ly to the Hun._____
fleet a - gain But don't let's be beast - ly to the

Hun._____

211

Sigh No More

from
SIGH NO MORE

Poor mournful lad-ies, are you weep-ing for a dream once dreamed?

Are you still list-en-ing for some re-mem-bered theme that

seemed ... To prom-ise hap-pi-ness and love and gen-tle years, ___ de-void of fears? Sweet mu - sic starts a-gain, lift up your hearts a-gain and dry, ___ ah, dry those tears. ___

REFRAIN *Not too slow, very legato*

Sigh no more, sigh no more. Grey clouds of

sor-row fill the sky no more. Cry no more,

Die no more, Those lit-tle deaths at part-ing, new life and new

love are start-ing, Sing a - gain, sing a - gain,

The win-ter's o - ver and it's spring a - gain. Joy is
your trou - ba - dour, Sweet and be - guil-ing lad - ies,
sigh no more, sigh no more, Sweet and be - guil-ing lad - ies,
sigh no more. more.

215

Matelot
from
SIGH NO MORE

Jean Lou-is Dom-en-ic sailed a - way Fur - ther than love could find him,
Jean Lou-is Dom-en-ic right or wrong Ev - er pur-sued a - new love,

rit.

Yet thro' the night He heard a light And gen-tle voice be-hind him say:— Mat-e-
Till in his brain There beat a strain He knew to be his true love song:— Mat-e-

rit.

REFRAIN (*Not too Slow*)

-lot— Mat - e - lot Where you go My thoughts go with you Mat - e -
-lot— Mat - e - lot Where you go My heart goes with you Mat - e -

-lot— Mat - e - lot. When you go down to the sea As you
-lot— Mat - e - lot. When you go down to the sea For a

217

gaze from a - far On the eve-ning star Wher - ev - er you may roam, You will re -
year and a day You may sail a - way And have no thought of me, Yet thro' the

- mem-ber the light Thro' the win - ter night That guides you safe - ly home. Tho' you
wind and the spray You will hear me say No love was ev - er free. You will

find Wo-men-kind to be frail, One love can-not fail— my son,
sigh when ho - riz - ons are clear, Some-thing that is dear to me

Till our days are done Mat - e - lot— Mat - e - lot. Where you
Can - not let me be Mat - e - lot— Mat - e - lot. Where you

go my thoughts go with you, Mat - e - lot— Mat - e - lot When you
go my heart goes with you, Mat - e - lot— Mat - e - lot When you

go down to the sea.   go down to the sea.

3rd REFRAIN

3. Mat - e - lot— Mat - e - lot Where you go my heart will fol-low Mat - e -

-lot— Mat - e - lot, When you go down to the see When there's

219

grief in the sky And the waves ride high My heart to yours will say, "You may be

sure that I'm true To my love for you, Tho' half the world a - way." Nev - er

mind If you find Oth - er charms, Here with - in my

arms— you'll sleep, Sail - or from the deep. Mat - e -

-lot— Mat - e - lot Where you go my heart will fol - low, Mat - e -

-lot— Mat - e - lot When you go—down to the sea. Ho____

Ho____ Ho____ Ho____ Ho____

Ho____ Ho.____

rit.

p

pp

221

Nina

from

SIGH NO MORE

Steady Rhumba tempo

Sen-o-ri - ta Ni - na_ from Ar-gen-
Sen-o-ri - ta Ni - na_ from Ar-gen-

-ti - na_ Knew all the ans - wers_Though all her rel-a-tives and friends were perfect
-ti - na_ des-pised the Tan - go_ Al-though she nev-er was a girl to let a

dan - cers___ She swore she'd nev - er dance a step un - til she
man - go___ She would-n't sac - ri - fice her prin - ci - ples for

died. She said 'I've seen too ma - ny Mov - ies___ And all they
sex. She look'd with scorn on the gy - ra - tions_ Of her re -

prove is Too i - di - o - tic._They all in - sist that South A - mer - i - ca's ex -
-la - tions Who danc'd the 'Con - ga'._ And swore that if she had to stand it an - y

-ot - ic_Where - as it could-n't be more bor - ing if it tried!'
long - er_ She'd lose all dig - ni - ty and wring their sil - ly necks!

She add - ed firm - ly that she ha - ted _ The sound of soft gui - tars _ be-side a
She said that frank-ly she was blind - ed _ To all their ov - er ad - ver-tised ro-

still la - goon, _ She al - so pos - i - tive - ly sta - ted _ That she could
-man - tic charms, _ And then she got more blood - y mind - ed _ And told them

not a - bide _ a 'South-ern Moon'. She said I hate to be pe -
where to put _ their 'Trop - ic Palms'. And she could not re - frain from

-dan - tic But I'm driv - en near - ly fran - tic When I see that un - ro -
say - ing That their i - di - ot - ic sway - ing And those damned 'gui - tar - ras'

224

-man-tic Sy - co-phan-tic lot of sluts.
play-ing Were an in - sult to her Race.

For - ev - er wrig-gl - ing their
And that she real - ly could-n't

guts
face

It drives me ab - so-lute - ly nuts.
Such in - ter-na-tion-al dis - grace!

She re - fused to be - gin the 'Be - guine' When they re - quest - ed it
She de - clined to be - gin the 'Be - guine' Tho' they be - sought her to

And she made an em - bar-rass-ing scene If an - y-one sug-ges - ted it,
And with lan-guage pro-fane and ob - scene She curs'd the man who taught her to

225

For she de - tes - ted it.
She curs'd Cole Por - ter too!

Though no one ev - er could be
From this it's fair - ly clear that

keen - er___ Than lit - tle Ni - na___ On quite a
Ni - na___ In her de - mean - our___ Was so of -

num - ber___ Of ve - ry el - ig - i - ble men who did the
fen - sive___ That when the ha - tred of her friends grew too in -

'Rhum - ba'___ When they pro - posed to her she sim - ply left them
-ten - sive___ She thought she'd bet - ter beat it while she had the

flat.
chance.

She said that love should be im-
Af - ter some trial and tri - bu-

rit.

-pul - sive___ But not con - vul - sive___ And syn - co-
-la - tion___ She reach'd the sta - tion___ And met a

a tempo

-pa - tion___ Had a dis - cour - ag - ing ef - fect on pro - cre-
sail - or___ Who had ac - quir'd a wood - en leg in Ven - e-

227

-a - tion__ And that she'd ra-ther read a book and that was that!
-zue - la__ And so she married him be-cause he *could-n't*

D.C. al 𝄋

2

dance!

CODA

There sure-ly nev-er could have been a__

More ir-rit-at-ing girl than Ni - na__ They nev-er speak in Ar-gen-

228

-ti - na___ Of this de-gen-er-ate 'Bam - bi - na'___

Who had the luck to find ro - mance

And res-o-lute-ly would-n't

da - - - - - - - - -

- - - nce!___ She would-n't dance!- Hola!!

229

I Wonder What Happened To Him

from
SIGH NO MORE

1. The In - dia that one read a - bout And
2. One can't de - ny that, by and large, Up-

may have been mis - led a - bout In one res - pect has kept it - self in -
-hold - ers of the Brit - ish Raj Don't shine in con - ver - sa - tion as a

-tact. _____ Though 'Puk - ka Sahib' tra - dit - ions may have
breed. _____ Though In - dian Arm - y of - fi - cers can

cracked And thinned, The good old In - dian arm - y's still a fact. That
read a bit, Their ver - bal wit — has rath - er run to seed. Their

fam - ous mon - u-ment - al man The 'Of - fi - cer and Gen - tle-man' Still
splen - did in - su-lar - i -ty And rog - uish joc - u-lar - i -ty Were

lives and breathes and func - tions from Bom - bay to Khat - man-du. _____ At
ech - o-ing through In - dia when Vic - tor - i - a was Queen. ____ In

231

an - y mo - ment one can glimpse Mat -ured or em - bry-on - ic 'Blimps' Vi-
res - taur-ants and din - ing-cars; In Mess - es, Clubs and ho - tel bars They

-vac-ious-ly spec - u-lat - ing as to what be-came of who! _____ Though
try to main-tain tra-dit - ion in the way it's al - ways been. _____ Though

East - ern sounds may fas - cin - ate your ear, _____ When
worlds may change and na - tions dis - ap - pear _____ A -

West meets West you're al - ways sure to hear— What -
-bove the shriek - ing cha - os you will hear— What -

1st & 3rd REFRAINS

-ev-er be-came of old Bag-ot?__ I hav-'n't seen him for a year.__ Is it
-ev-er be-came of old Tuck-er?__ Have you heard an-y word of young Mills__ Who

true that old Briggs had to mar-ry that Fag-got He met in the Vale of Kash-mir___ Have you
rup-tured him-self at the end of a 'Chuk-ka' And had to. be sent to the hills?__ They

had an-y news Of that chap in the 'Blues' Was it Pros-ser or Pye-croft or Pym?__ He was
say that young Lees had a go of 'D. Ts'. And his hopes of pro-mot-ion are slim.__ Ac-

sta-tioned at Sim-la or was it Ben-gal? I know he got tight at a ball in Ne-pal And
-cord-ing to Stubbs who's a bit of a louse The sil-ly young blight-er went out on a 'souse' And

233

wrote sev-'ral four let-ter words on the wall! I won-der what hap-pened to
took two old tarts in-to Gov-ern-ment house. I won-der what hap-pened to

ad lib.

him! What-
him! What-

2nd & 4th REFRAINS

-ev-er be-came of old Shel-ley?___ Is it true that young Forbes was cash-iered.___ For
-ev-er be-came of old Arch-ie?___ I hear he de-part-ed this life___ Af-ter

rid-ing, quite nude, on a push bike thro' Del-hi The day the new Vice-roy ap-peared?___ Has
round-ing up ten sa-cred cows in Kar-a-chi To wel-come the Gov-er-nor's wife,___ D'you re-

234

an-y-one heard of that bloke in the 'Third' Was it South-er-by, Sedgwick or Sim?___ They
-mem-ber Mun-roe in the 'P. A. V. O.' He was tall-ish and men-tal-ly dim.___ That

had him thrown out of a club in Bom-bay For, a-part from his Mess-bills ex-ceed-ing his pay, He
talk of 'He-red-i-ty' can't be quite true He was dropped on his head by his Ay-ah at two, I pre-

took to pig-stick-ing in *quite* the wrong way. I wonder what hap-pened to him!
-sume that by now he'll have reached 'G. H. Q.' I'm

D.C.al 𝄋

sure that's what's hap-pened to him!

235

That is the
End of the News

from

SIGH NO MORE

1. We are told___ ve - ry loud - ly and of - ten To lift up our
2. We are told___ that it's dis - mal and drear - y To air our des -

hearts
- pairs

We are told___ that good hu - mour will
We are told___ to be gal - lant and

soft - en Fate's cru - el - lest darts
cheer - y And ban - ish our cares

So how - ev - er bad our do - mes - tic trou - bles may
So when for - tune gives us a cup of hem - lock to

be
quaff

meno mosso

We just shake with a -
We just give a slight

-muse - ment and sing with glee.
hic - cup and laugh laugh laugh.

poco rall.

tenuto

237

Heigh - ho   Mum's had those pains a - gain   Gran-ny's in   bed with her
Heigh - ho   ev -'ry-thing's fear-ful   We   do wish that   Vi   was a
Heigh - ho   what a   cat - as - tro - phe   Grand-fa - ther's   brain is   be -

va - ri - cose veins a-gain   Ev -'ry-one's   gay be-cause dear cou-sin Flor-rie Was
lit - tle more cheer-ful The   on - ly re - sult of her last op-er - a - tion Has
-gin-ning to   at - ro - phy   Last Sun-day   night af - ter eat-ing an   ap - ple He

run down on   Sat - ur - day   night by   a   lor - ry We're   so   glad
been gales of   wind at the   least pro - vo - ca - tion Now   don't   laugh,
made a   rude   noise in the   Meth - o - dist   Cha - pel   Good   egg,

El - sie's mis - car-riage Oc-curred on   the   Wed-nes-day   af - ter her mar-riage When
poor Mrs__   Ma - son Was wash-ing some smalls in   the   la - va-tory ba - sin When
dear lit - tle   Dor-is Has just been ex - pelled for as - sault-ing Miss Mor-ris

Al - bert fell down all The steps of the Town Hall He got three bad cuts and a
that old cor - ro - ded Gas heat-er ex - plo-ded And blew her smack in - to the
Both of her sis-ters are cov-ered in blis-ters From stand-ing a - bout in the

bruise We're 'de - light - ed To be a - ble to say We're un -
Mews We're in clo - ver Un - cle George is in clink For re -
queues We've been done in, By that mort-gage fore - clos-ure And

- a - ble to pay Off our debts We're ex - ci - ted Be - cause
- fus-ing to work for the war Now it's o - ver Aunt - ie
fa - ther went out on a blind He got run in, For in -

R.H.

Per - cy's got mange and we've run up a bill at the vets.
Maud seems to think He'll be far bet-ter placed than be - fore.
- de - cent ex - pos - ure And ev - er so hea - vi - ly fined.

239

Three cheers, Er-nie's got boils a-gain Ev-'ry-thing's cov-ered in
What fun, dear lit-tle Sid-ney Pro-duced a spec-tac-u-lar
Heigh - ho Hi-did-dle did-dle Aunt Is-a-bel's shin-gles have

oint-ment and oils a-gain Now he's had sev-en, so God's in his
stone in his kid-ney He's had e-lev-en So God's in his
met in the mid-dle She's bur-ied in Dev-on So God's in his

hea-ven And that is the end of the news.
hea-ven And that is the end of the
hea-ven And that is the end of the

sfz

news.
news.

sfz

240

This is a Changing World

from

PACIFIC 1860

Andante con moto

The world was young So man-y, man-y years a-go ___ The passage of time must show ___ Some trac-es of change. Love songs once sung Much laugh-ter, man-y tears Have ech-oed down the years, The

past is old and strange._____ Each wan-ing moon, All

dawns that rise, all suns that set _____ Change like the tides that

flow a - cross the sands. _____ Each lit - tle tune That

fills our hearts with vague re-gret,_____ Each lit - tle love du-et _____ Fades in our

242

hands. _____ Don't stray a - mong the mo-ments that have fled, New

days are just a - head, New words are still un - said.

Tempo di Valse

REFRAIN

This is a chang - ing world, my
This is a chang - ing world, my

mf rit. *a tempo*

dear, New songs are sung, new stars ap - pear.
dear, New dreams are dreamed, new dawns ap - pear.

Though we grow old - er year by year Our hearts can still be gay. _____
Passion's a feck - less cav - a - lier Who loves and rides a - way. _____

Young love at best is a pass - ing phase,
Time will per - suade you to laugh at grief,

Charm - ing and fool - ish and blind. _____
Time is your ten - der - est friend. _____

There may be hap - pi - er, wis - er days When youth is far be -
Life may be lone - ly and joy be brief But ev - 'ry - thing must

-hind. _____ Where are the snows of yes - ter - year? When
end. _____ Love is a charm - ing sou - ven - ir When

Win - ter's done and Spring is here? No re-
day is done and night draws near. No re -

- grets are worth a tear, We're liv-ing in a chang-ing world, my
- grets are worth a tear, We're liv-ing in a chang-ing world, my

dear.

dear. _____

245

His Excellency Regrets

from

PACIFIC 1860

Oh tell us please___ en-tire-ly con-fi-den-tial-ly___

___ How A. D. C's ___ are trained in so-cial grace ___ Its aw-fully

brave dai-ly to be called up-on to save___ His

Ex - cel - len - cy's face! _____

An - y ex - plan - a - tions of the du - ties of an A. D. C.

Prove the com - pli - ca - tions that are rife at Government House.

Cer - tain si - tu - a - tions we could nev - er let a la - dy see

247

There are strange vi - bra - tions in the life at Gov-ern-ment House.

Truth is of - ten sa - cri-ficed for rea - sons of di - plo - ma - cy

That of course we un - der-stand but all the same it must be grand to

be so suave, so calm so dig - ni - fied ! If you

knew what all that sig - ni - fied we _____

_____ who break the ninth com - mand - ment ev - 'ry day _____

Would hang our heads in shame and say _____ For - give _____ we have _____ to

live _____ Of - fi - cial - ly on feet of clay _____

Ev - 'ry mi-nute were made to sin it is real - ly ve-ry de-

-praved   But   to Hell with the lies we tell His   Ex - cel - len - cy's

Hon - our must   be   saved

His

250

REFRAIN

Ex-cel-len-cy re - grets _____ That ow-ing to an at-tack of Gout He

real - ly dare not ven-ture out on Sa-tur-day to dine. _____ His

Ex-cel-len-cy re - grets _____ That ow-ing to doc-tors or-ders he can-

-not at-tend the Mis-sion tea And al - so must de - cline _____ Your

251

kind in - vi - ta - tion For Wed - nes - day week.＿＿ A

slight op - er - a - tion And poor cir - cu - la - tion Com-

-bined with a weed - y phy - sique ＿＿＿ Has made him un - a - ble to

speak ＿ All this in ad - di - tion to what ＿ The doc-tors discribe as a

'Clot'_____ which may dis-ap-pear by the end of the year But

may, ve-ry pos-si-bly not!___ His Ex-cel-len-cy re - grets___ That

ow-ing to his ex - alt - ed state He can no more as - so - ci-ate With

am - ia-ble bru - nettes. Walk up walk up we're

253

will-ing to take your bets ____ That that's one of the prin-ci-pal things His

Ex-cel-len-cy re-grets! So now we know____ a-bout the di-plo-

-ma-tic Corps ____ How it can so____ Cor-rupt the soul of

youth _____ What hap-pens if____ some day you give the

waiting world a whiff ____ Of plain un - var - nished

truth? _____ His Ex-cel-len-cy re - grets ____ That,

fail-ing a bet - ter a - li - bi He must ad-mit he'd rath - er die Than

op - en your Ba - zaar. ____ His Ex-cel-len-cy re - grets ____ That,

255

lack-ing e-nough of-fi-cial scope, He can't dis-band the Band of Hope No

mat-ter where they are. _____ He frank-ly des-pis - es

the peo-ple he rules _____ His gorge al - so ris - es when

giv-ing the priz - es At co-e-du-ca-tion-al schools _____ to

rows of il-li-te-rate fools _____ And if you should write in the book _____ He'll give you a murd-er-ous look _____ For it ru-ins his day to be tak-en a-way From his rod and his line and his hook! _____ His Ex-cel-len-cy re-grets _____ He

257

has-n't e-nough to run the house or pay the staff or feed a mouse up-

-on the pay he gets. Heigh ho Heigh ho he's up to his ears in

debts _____ But that's one of the least of the things His

Ex - cel - len - cy re - grets. _____

258

Bright Was The Day

from
PACIFIC 1860

morn - ing when I woke the light was clear in the sky, A

sweet wind mur-mur'd thro' the trees. _____ A

sing-ing bird was sing-ing ve-ry near in the sky,— And in the

breeze_____ which drove the clouds so gai - ly

cresc.

mf rall.   *colla voce*

by_____ I thought I heard a diff -'rent

rall.   *colla voce*

note,_____ a lit - tle sigh_____ Which seem'd to

rall.

say _____ This is your day, _____ Be care-ful, please, _____ Be care-ful,

please! ___ Don't let this light en-chant-ment fade a - way, _____ This is your

day. This morn-ing when I woke, I seem'd to

know in my heart,_ That some new hap-pi-ness was near. _____ I

261

wait - ed for this un - ex - pect - ed glow in my heart___ To dis - ap-

-pear._____ But strange to say it would not

rall.   *colla voce*

go, _____ And as the mo-ments hur - ried

rall.   *colla voce*

by, _____ it seem'd to grow. _____ If, as you

say_____ This is your day,_____ Kind ca-va-lier,_____ kind ca-va-

-lier,_____ We'll try to let this brief en-chant-ment

stay_____ Just for to-day_____ This is your day._____ Though

we_____ may nev-er meet a-gain,__There'll nev-er be_____ a day so

sweet a - gain.___ Deep in my heart, no mat-ter what the troubled

years may bring, ___ A se-cret voice ___ will ev - er sing. ___

Tempo di Valse Moderato

rall.   *rit.*   *mf*

REFRAIN

1. Bright was the day when you came to me,
2. Here in the sun-shine I came to you,

mf

Some-one had whis-pered your name to me. Some-one had told me how
Some-one had whis-pered my name to you. Some po - tent ma - gic im -

264

fair you were, Then at last— there you were! Light was the
-pelled me here, Touched my heart— held me here! Dreams long for-

mu-sic that played for me, You were the song Des-ti-ny had made for
-got-ten re-vive a-gain, Sud-den-ly life seems to be a-live a-

me. I heard the mel-o-dy start_____ Del-i-cate-ly,
-gain. I heard the mel-o-dy too_____ Beck-on-ing me,

del-i-cate-ly in my heart.
beck-on-ing me here to you.

The Fifties

From 'Ace of Clubs', 1950. 'Ace of Clubs' was a musical comedy written in an idiom entirely different from my other musical plays. The action was laid chiefly in a Soho night club, in which Pat Kirkwood was the star, Pinkie Leroy, and Graham Payn the sailor who fell in love with her. The story was full of gangsters, black marketeers, tough chorus girls, stolen jewellery, etc. There were no vocalized opening choruses or finales, no quartettes and only one trio, 'Three Juvenile Delinquents', which invariably brought the house down at every performance. It was brilliantly performed by John Warwick, Peter Tuddenham and Colin Kemball. They looked degraded little·brutes and were exceedingly funny. A very disgruntled old magistrate wrote a letter to a newspaper protesting that not only was the song vulgar but it was also an incentive to crime! I cannot help wondering whether or not he was one of those who missed the point of 'Don't Let's be Beastly to the Germans' a few years earlier. The tone of his letter was almost identically obtuse. I have suffered many slings and arrows in my life from enraged moralists. I do wish they'd shut up. As far as I am concerned their cause is a lost one from the outset.

'Why Does Love Get in the Way?' is a fairly straight song in 'beguine' tempo.

'Sail Away' is good, I think. It has a nice swing to it and the tune is catchy.

'I Like America' has an effective lyric, but unfortunately, owing to its musical structure, the last phrase is not sufficiently telling.

'Josephine' is a comedy number, not remarkable but quite funny. Pat Kirkwood sang it extremely well.

'Chase Me Charlie', based on the old music hall 'Oompa-pa', is a gay song about a cat. I always envisaged in my mind someone like Lottie Collins or Florrie Forde swinging up and down the stage in sequins and belting it over. Pat Kirkwood could not be said to resemble either of these ladies, but she put it across in her own way very effectively.

Don't Make Fun of the Fair

From 'The Lyric Revue', 1951. This song was written as a satire. It was sung successfully as a quartette in 'The Lyric Revue' and as a solo by me at the Café de Paris. It is neither pro-German, pro-Russian nor particularly anti-British. I do not believe that it has been an incentive to crime and it is too much to hope that it could in any way be a deterrent to bureaucratic idiocy. It is a jolly number but, alas! too topical to live on in the hearts of men.

Why Does Love Get in the Way

from

ACE OF CLUBS

VERSE

Sud-den-ly my world has al-tered, Sud-den-ly my step has fal-tered,

Com-mon sense has flown, Here I am a-lone, Cop-ing with these new sen-sa-tions,

Dark des-pairs and wild e-la-tions, E-ros with his bow— has laid me low.

REFRAIN

Why does love _____ get in the way so? _____

What have I done that the son-of-a-gun should pick on

me? _____ A lit-tle while a-go my heart was se-rene and

bright, Ev-'ry-thing seemed all right, Now I've been

struck by a charge of dy - - na - mite. Why does love_____

lead one a - stray so,_____ Tell me why_____

___ I want to laugh, I want to cry._____ I was

gay as a spar-row, Till Cu-pids ar-row punc-tured this per-fect day, Why does

love _____ get in the way? _____

VERSE

Ev - 'ry - thing is blown to blaz - es, or - din - 'ry fam - il - iar phras - es

mp colla voce

Seem to mean much more Than they did be - fore. Col - ours look a great deal bright - er,

Black is black-er, white is whit-er, Ev-'ry sight and sound has changed a-round.

REFRAIN

Why does love _____ get in the way so? _____ Why should it

fret and completely up - set my peace of mind? _____ A lit-tle while a-go my

heart was se-rene and gay Ev-'ry-thing seemed O - Kay.

273

And now I sud-den-ly find I've lost my way. Why does love lead one a - stray so? Why the Hell Should I be caught with-in its spell? Life was quite un-en-chant-ed, All that I want-ed,

Sail Away

from

ACE OF CLUBS

Allegro moderato

When a sail - or goes to sea   Though   he leaves his love be - hind
Love   is meant to make us glad,   Love   can make the world go round

Time   and Tide will set him free   From the grief in - side   him.
Love   can drive you rav - ing mad,   Tor - ment and up - set   you.

Sea   and sky will ease his heart,   Reg - u-late his trou-bled mind
Love   can give your heart   a   jolt   But   phil-o - so-phers have found

Ev - 'ry sail - or   has   a   chart,   And   a   star   to   guide   him
That   it's wise   to   do   a   bolt   When   it starts   to   get   you

home.   _____   When the
down.   _____   When your

277

REFRAIN

storm clouds are rid-ing through a win - ter sky, Sail a - way____
life seems too dif-fi - cult to rise a - bove Sail a - way____

____ Sail a - way._____ When the love - light is fad-ing in your
____ Sail a - way._____ When your heart feels as drear-y as a

sweet - heart's eye Sail a - way_____ Sail a - way.____
worn out glove Sail a - way_____ Sail a - way.____

____ When you feel your song is or - ches-tra -ted wrong
____ But when soon or late You re - cogn-ize your Fate

Why should you pro - long your stay?_____ When the wind and the
That will be your great great day_____ On the wings of the

wea - ther blow your dreams sky high Sail a - way Sail a -
morn - ing with your own true love Sail a - way Sail a -

1
- way Sail a - way._____ When you
- way Sail a -

2
- way._____

D.C.

279

Josephine

from
ACE OF CLUBS

§ Tempo di Valse moderato

VERSE

1. The la - dy was beau-ti-ful the la - dy was dark, She was-n't too du - ti-ful but still left her mark — On vol - umes of his-to-ry and

2. What ev - er she near-ly did from five to fif - teen, We know that she real-ly did be - gin the Be - guine, On first meet-ing Bon-a-parte she

thou-sands of cheques And all through the mys-te-ry of 'Ole Deb-bil Sex.
mur-mured "Hell's Bells!" You let down the tone a-part from ev-'ry-thing-else!

REFRAIN

Jo - se - phine _____ Jo - se - phine _____ from the first was
Jo - se - phine _____ Jo - se - phine _____ ve - ry sel - dom

ra - ther chic _____ As a tot _____ She would trot _____
lost con - trol, _____ Though her wit _____ Was a bit _____

_ Through the Is - land of Mar - ti - nique. _____ Her
_ O - ver sea - soned with "Sauce Cre - ole." _____ She

for - tune was told by an a - ged crone Who pro - phe - sied
ve - ry soon mar - ried this short young man Who talked a - bout

fame and ro - mance, _____ And who hissed in her ear the out -
sol - diers all day, _____ But who was - n't a - bove mak - ing

- rage - ous i - dea that she'd al - so be em - press of France. _____
pas - sion - ate love in a coarse, ra - ther Cor - si - can way. _____

_ Jo - se - phine _____ Jo - se - phine _____ Had with
_ Jo - se - phine _____ was - n't keen _____ And Na -

282

men a set rou - tine,_____ And the peo - ple who
-po - leon made a scene,_____ He said "Dear, your un-

thought her tech - nique was self taught did - n't know Jo - se-
-will - ing be - hav - iour is kill - ing the show Jo - se-

To 2nd Verse   D.S. 2   REFRAIN

-phine.   -phine,"   Jo - se - phine,_____ Jo - se-

-phine._____ Though a queen re - mained at home,_____ While her

lord _____ was a-broad _____ send-ing post-cards, in code, from Rome. _____ He of-ten ap-peared with a three day beard from Aus-tri-a, Po-land or Spain, _____ And one dread-ful night he ar-rived ra-ther tight hav-ing messed up the Rus-sian cam-

-paign. _____ Jo - se - phine, _____ turn-ing green _____ cried,"What-
-ev - er does this mean?" _____ Then Na - po - leon said,"Whoops! I have
lost all my troops in the snow   Jo - sie   Oh,
Jo - sie, snow   Jo - se - phine!" _____

Chase Me Charlie

from

ACE OF CLUBS

Bright Valse tempo

1. When it's late ____ and the world is sleep - ing,
2. Ev - 'ry night ____ at a - bout e - lev - en,

Our lit - tle black cat, No big - ger than that,
Our lit - tle cat knows, Our lit - tle cat goes,

Has a date ___ which she's keen on keep - ing.
Quick as light ___ To her pri - vate heav - en.

No use dis - suad - ing her, She's ser - e - nad - ing her
No use re - strain - ing her, She's set on gain - ing her

Beau, _____ In the gar - den be -
prize, _____ With her am - our - ous

-low. _____ She sings "Oh won't you
cries _____ Hyp - no - tiz - ing him

rall.

REFRAIN

1 Chase me, Char-lie, Chase me, Char-lie,
2 Chase me, Char-lie, Chase me, Char-lie,

O-ver the gar-den wall. _____ I'd like to
O-ver the gar-den wall. _____ Why should we

wan-der for miles and miles, Wreathed in smiles Out on the
care if the neigh-bours shout, Please come out Lets fool a-

tiles with you, Chase me, Char-lie, Chase me, Char-lie,
-bout a bit, Chase me, Char-lie, Chase me, Char-lie,

288

don't be a - fraid to fall, _____ Love in the moon light can
I'll be your all in all, _____ If you'll ap - pear and be

be sub - lime, Now's the time Char - lie,
gay with me, Play with me Stay with

I'm wait - ing for you if you'll on - ly climb,
me? A - ny sug - ges-tions o - kay with me,

O - ver the gar - den wall.
O - ver the gar - den wall. _____

Chase me, Char - lie, Chase me, Char - lie, O - ver the gar - den wall. _____ Why not give in to the joys of Spring, Have a fling Why are you lin - ger - ing? Chase me, Char - lie, Chase me, Char - lie,

290

This is my fi - nal call, _____ Pus - sy - cat,

Pus - sy - cat don't be coy, Jump for joy Oi! Oi!

Oi! Straight - en your whisk - ers and 'At - ta Boy,'

O - ver the gar - den wall. _____

I Like America

from
ACE OF CLUBS

Tell us sail-or Tell us please for we're ter-ri-bly keen to know What it's

like to be fan-cy free ___ Foot-loose on the roll-ing sea?

Chi-na girl chop-chop Gay Malt-ese Hot Mommas from Mex-i - co If

you'll for-give a crude re-mark and don't re-sent a rude re-mark I'll

let you in-to a se-cret Well? They're all a-like in the dark There

must have been some place you've seen su - pe-ri-or to the rest? As a

293

matter of fact with pol - i - ti - cal tact I like A - mer - i - ca

Slowly   *con spirito*

best. There's a good time a - com-in' on de ole plan - ta - tion for a

jol- ly Jack Tar has just con-fessed that he likes A-mer - i - ca best. I

don't care for Chi - na, Ja - pan's far too small   I've rum-bled the
loathed ev' - ry ac - re From Cannes to Can - ton,   I al - so de -

rit.

a tempo

294

295

REFRAIN

Slower (*Steady tempo*)

I like A - mer - i - ca   I have played a - round   Ev - 'ry
I like A - mer - i - ca   I have tra-velled far   From Nor-

slap - py hap - py hunt - ing ground But I   find   A -
-thum - ber-land to Zan - zi - bar But I   find   A -

-mer - i - ca   O - kay.
-mer - i - ca   O - kay.

I've been a - bout a bit   but I must ad - mit   That I
I've roamed the Span-ish Main,   Ea - ten su - gar cane   But I

did-n't know the half of it till I hit the U. S.
ne-ver tas-ted cel-lo-phane till I struck the U. S.

A.
A.

No like-ly lass in Bos-ton, Mass, from
All de-le-gates in South-ern States Are

pas-sion will re-coil _____ In Dal-las Tex they
ner-vy and dis-traught _____ In New Or-leans the

talk of sex But on-ly think of oil. _____ New
wrought-iron screens Are dread-f'lly o-ver-wrought. _____ Be-

Jer-sey dames go up in flames if some-one men-tions bed In Chi-
-neath each tree In Ten-ne-see E - ro - tic books are read, And when

-ca-go Ill-i-nois An - y girl who meets a boy Gig-gles and shoots him
al - li - ga-tors thud Through the Mis-si-si-pi mud, Sex rears its ug - ly

dead But I like A - mer-i-ca Its so-
head! But I like A - mer-i-ca Its sim-

-ci-e-ty of-fers in-fi-nite va-ri-e-ty And come what
-pli-ci-ty And its pas-sion for pub-li-ci-ty And come what

298

may   I shall re-turn some day   To the good old
may   Give me a hol - i - day   In the good old

1
U.   S.   A.   I've
U.   S.   **2** A.

pp

Hey - hey.   Hey - hey.

cresc.

sfz

Don't Make Fun of the Fair

from

THE LYRIC REVUE

Brightly (*not too fast*)

We're
We've

proud to say in ev-'ry way we're or - din - a - ry folk_____ But
nev - er been ex - act - ly keen on show-ing off or swank_____ But

please ob-serve we still pre-serve our stur-dy hearts of oak.___ Alas they say that gay dis-play means mon-ey in the bank.___ We'll

-though as ser-vants of the state we may have been co-erced___ As
make the dread-ful wel-kin ring from Penge to John-O-Groats___ And

we've been told to cel-e-brate we'll cel-e-brate or burst.___ Though
cheer, and laugh, and shout and sing be-fore we cut our throats.___ We

while we brag our shoul-ders sag be-neath a heav-y yoke___ We
know we're caught and must sup-port this pa-tri-o-tic prank___ And

all get ter-ri-bly heat-ed if it's treat-ed as a joke.
though we'd ra-ther have shot our-selves we've got our-selves to thank.

REFRAIN

So Don't make fun of the fes-ti-val Don't make fun of the fair, We
So Don't make fun of the fes-ti-val Don't make fun of the fair, We
So Don't make fun of the fes-ti-val Don't make fun of the fair, We
So Don't make fun of the fes-ti-val Don't make fun of the fair, We

down-trod-den Brit-ish must learn to be skit-tish and give an im-pres-sion of
must pull to-geth-er in spite of the wea-ther that damp-ens our spi-rits and
must have a look at a cook-er-y book to pre-vent us from spreading a-
mus-n't look glum when the vi-si-tors come and dis-cov-er our cup-board is

dev-il-may-care. To the wide wide world _____
straigh-tens our hair. Let the peo-ple sing _____
-larm and des-pair. We can serve whale steaks _____
ev-er so bare. We must cheer boys cheer _____

We'll sing "God for Har-ry" ____ And if it turns out al - right.
Ev - en though they shi - ver ____ Ro - ses red and no - ses mauve.
When the wea - ther's hot - ter ____ And in place of en - tre - cotes.
Look as though we love it ____ And if it should be a bust

Knight Ger - ald Bar - ry. ____ Clear the na - tion - al decks my lads
Ov - er the ri - ver. ____ Though the ar - e - a's fair - ly small
What's wrong with ot - ter? ____ Greet the ga - la with fer - vence boys
just rise a - bove it. ____ Take a nip from your bran - dy flask

Ev - 'ry one of us counts, Grab your trav-el - er's cheques my lads And
Climb Dis - cov - er - y's Dome, Take a snooze in the con - cert hall At
Learn to dance in the dark, Build the Sun-day ob - ser - vance boys A
Scream and ca - per and shout, Don't give an - y - one time to ask

pray that none of them bounce. ____ Boys and Girls come out to play
least it's warm - er than home. ____ March a - bout in fun - ny hats
shrine in Bat - ter - sea Park. ____ Cross your fin - gers hold your thumbs
What the Hell it's a - bout. ____ Face the fu - ture un - dis - mayed

303

Ev - 'ry day in ev - 'ry way   Help the tour - ist
Show the for - eign dip - lo - mats   That our pro - le -
Blow your trum - pets roll your drums   Ev - en if no -
Pray for fur - ther Mar - shall aid   Have the toast from

to de - fray All that's un - der - writ - ten.___ Sell your ra - tions and
- ta - ri - ats Mil - der than a kit - ten.___ We be - lieve in the
- bo - dy comes Don't be con-science smit - ten.___ If no ov - er - seas
Cav - al - cade Dras - ti - c'lly re - writ - ten.___ Peace and dig - ni - ty

ov - er - charge, And don't let an - y - one sab - o - tage. Our
right to strike, But know we've blood - y - well got to like Our
trade ap - pears We'll have to work for a thou - sand years To
we may lack, But wave a jol - ly Trades U - nion Jack. Hoo -

own dear fes - ti - val of Bri - tain.___   own dear

fes - ti - val of Bri - tain._____ pay for the fes - ti - val of

Bri - tain._____ -ray for the fes - ti - val we'll

pray for the fes - ti - val Hoo - ray for the fes - ti - val of

Bri - tain._____

305

Three Juvenile Delinquents

from

ACE OF CLUBS

1. Three Juv-en-ile De-lin-quents, Juv-en-ile De-lin-quents, Hap-py as can
2. Three Juv-en-ile De-lin-quents, Juv-en-ile De-lin-quents, Hap-py as can
3. Three Juv-en-ile De-lin-quents, Juv-en-ile De-lin-quents, Hap-py as can
4. Three Juv-en-ile De-lin-quents, Juv-en-ile De-lin-quents, Ev-'ry now and
5. Three Juv-en-ile De-lin-quents, Juv-en-ile De-lin-quents, Hap-py as can

be— we Waste no time On the where-fores and whys of it,
be— we Hit and run For the thrill and the sport of it,
be— we Lick our chops When we read what they write of us,
then— when Kind old cranks Men-tion An-gels of Light to us,
be— we Break our backs To a-chieve pop-u-lar-i-ty,

We like crime And that's a-bout the size of it. Peo-ple say that
Nice clean fun, And that's the long and short of it. Dear old la-dies
All the cops___ Hate the blood-y sight of us. Once we pinched a
We say 'Thanks,_ Don't for-get to write to us'. Now-a-days the
Three sharp whacks,_ Faith and Hope and Cha-ri-ty. Once we knocked a

films de-mor-a-lize us;   Lead us to a life of   shame,
oft-en get the va-pours   When we meet them af - ter   dark   (Whoo!)
Ca - dil-lac and drove her   From the Mar - ble Arch   to   Kew,
young-er gen-er-a-tion   Nev-er has to face brute   force,
pair of sil-ly sluts out   Just be-hind the 'Horse and   Plough',

Men - tal   doc-tors   try to civ-il-ize us,   Psy-cho an-al-yse   us,
Then next   day we   read a-bout our ca-pers,   In the dai-ly pa-pers,
Hit a   fat old   geez-er in a Ro-ver,   Fair-ly bowled her o-ver,
Some old Judge in-   stead of fla-gel-la-tion   Puts us on-pro-ba-tion
Dragged them round to   where the rail-ing juts   out,   Bel-low-ing their guts out,

Bli-mey what a game!   They don't know how to   treat us, For if they should
Bli-mey what a lark!   We thrill the Sun-day   read-ers, But the sil-ly
Bli-mey what a do!   We said 'You must-n't   fuss dear, There's a love-ly
Bli-mey what a sauce!   Last night we got an   ear-ful From a rath-er
Bli-mey what a row!   We had to cosh 'em   pro-per, Then we saw a

308

beat us, That would nev-er do; When they say 'Go stead-y' We've the an-swer read-y—
bleed-ers Have-n't got a clue; When the Judge says 'Cho-key' We say O - key - do-key—
bus dear, Num-ber twen-ty - two, If we've bruised your bon-net Stick a plas-ter on it—
tear-ful Cler - gy-man we knew,When he turned the sobs on We re-plied 'With nobs on'—
cop-per Start-ing to pur-sue, So we cried, Vi - bra - to 'How's your old to - ma-to'—

1. 2. 3. 4

And the same to you!

Last time

same to you!

Appendix

NOTES ON NOËL COWARD MUSICAL PRODUCTIONS

LONDON CALLING
Revue by Ronald Jeans and Noël Coward
Music by Noël Coward and Philip Braham
Presented by André Charlot
September 4, 1923
Duke of York's Theatre
Principals:—
        Gertrude Lawrence
        Maisie Gay
        Tubby Edlin
        Noël Coward

ON WITH THE DANCE
Revue by Noël Coward
Music by Philip Braham and Noël Coward
Presented by Charles B. Cochran
April 30, 1925
London Pavilion
Principals:—
        Alice Delysia
        Leonide Massine
        Hermione Baddeley
        Douglas Byng

THIS YEAR OF GRACE
Revue Book, Lyrics and Music by Noël Coward
Presented by Charles B. Cochran
March 22, 1928
London Pavilion

THIS YEAR OF GRACE *(contd.)*

Principals:—
    Jessie Matthews
    Maisie Gay
    Tilly Losch
    Sonnie Hale
    Douglas Byng

THIS YEAR OF GRACE

Presented by Arch. Selwyn and Charles B. Cochran
November 7, 1928
Selwyn Theatre, New York
Principals:—
    Beatrice Lillie
    Noël Coward
    Florence Desmond
    Madeleine Gibson

BITTER SWEET

Operette. Written and composed by Noël Coward
Presented by Charles B. Cochran
July 18, 1929
His Majesty's Theatre
Principals:—
    Peggy Wood
    Ivy St. Helier
    George Metaxa

BITTER SWEET

Presented by Florenz Ziegfeld and Charles B. Cochran
November 5, 1929
Ziegfeld Theatre, New York
Principals:—
    Evelyn Laye
    Gerald Nodin
    Mireille

CAVALCADE

Play by Noël Coward
Presented by Charles B. Cochran
October 13, 1931
Theatre Royal, Drury Lane
Principals:—
    Mary Clare
    Irene Browne

WORDS AND MUSIC

Revue. Book, Lyrics and Music by Noël Coward
Presented by Charles B. Cochran
September 16, 1932
Adelphi Theatre

312

WORDS AND MUSIC   Principals:—
    (*contd.*)

                              Ivy St. Helier
                              Joyce Barbour
                              Doris Hare
                              Steffi Duna
                              Rita Lyle
                              Romney Brent
                              John Mills

CONVERSATION PIECE   Operette. Written and composed by Noël Coward
Presented by Charles B. Cochran
February 16, 1934
His Majesty's Theatre
Principals:—
           Yvonne Printemps
           Noël Coward
           Irene Browne
           Heather Thatcher
           Louis Hayward
           Moya Nugent

TO-NIGHT AT 8.30   Nine one-act plays by Noël Coward
Presented by John C. Wilson
January 9, 1936
Phoenix Theatre
Principals:—
           Gertrude Lawrence
           Noël Coward

TO-NIGHT AT 8.30   Presented by John C. Wilson
November 24, 1936
National Theatre, New York
Principals:—
           Gertrude Lawrence
           Noël Coward

OPERETTE   Operette. Written and composed by Noël Coward
Presented by John C. Wilson
March 16, 1938
His Majesty's Theatre
Principals:—
           Peggy Wood
           Fritzi Massary
           Irene Vanbrugh
           Griffith Jones

SET TO MUSIC	Revue. Book, Lyrics and Music by Noël Coward
	Presented by John C. Wilson
	January 18, 1939
	Music Box Theatre, New York
	Principals:—
	Beatrice Lillie
	Richard Haydn
SIGH NO MORE	Revue. Book, Lyrics and Music by Noël Coward
	Presented by H. M. Tennent and John C. Wilson
	August 22, 1945
	Piccadilly Theatre
	Principals:—
	Cyril Ritchard
	Madge Elliott
	Joyce Grenfell
	Graham Payn
PACIFIC 1860	Musical Romance by Noël Coward
	Presented by Prince Littler
	December 19, 1946
	Theatre Royal, Drury Lane
	Principals:—
	Mary Martin
	Graham Payn
	Sylvia Cecil
ACE OF CLUBS	Musical Play. Written and composed by Noël Coward
	Presented by Tom Arnold
	July 7, 1950
	Cambridge Theatre
	Principals:—
	Pat Kirkwood
	Graham Payn
	Sylvia Cecil